KT-559-593

30131 05735723 5
LONDON BOROUGH OF BARNET

SOME BODY TO LOVE

BY THE SAME AUTHOR

Ex and the City

Running Like a Girl

Leap In

ALEXANDRA HEMINSLEY

Some Body to Love

A FAMILY STORY

Chatto & Windus
LONDON

1 3 5 7 9 10 8 6 4 2

Chatto & Windus, an imprint of Vintage,
20 Vauxhall Bridge Road,
London SW1V 2SA

Chatto & Windus is part of the Penguin Random House group of companies whose addresses can be found at global.penguinrandomhouse.com

First published by Chatto & Windus in 2021

penguin.co.uk/vintage

A CIP catalogue record for this book is available from the British Library

ISBN 9781784743079

Typeset in 11/16 pt Adobe Garamond
by Integra Software Services Pvt. Ltd, Pondicherry

Printed and bound in Great Britain by Clays Ltd, Elcograf S.p.A.

The authorised representative in the EEA is Penguin Random House Ireland, Morrison Chambers, 32 Nassau Street, Dublin D02 YH68.

Penguin Random House is committed to a sustainable future for our business, our readers and our planet. This book is made from Forest Stewardship Council® certified paper.

For Damian and Mike:
I am as blessed with my logical family as with my biological one.

Love does not begin and end the way we seem to think it does.
Love is a battle, love is a war, love is a growing up.

James Baldwin

AUTHOR'S NOTE

This is my story, but of course it overlaps with that of my immediate family. I have tried to find the right balance between living an open and honest life and affording them their privacy. As such, I have not used full names but initials for those closest to me.

In the first half of the book I have avoided using male pronouns when referring to D. They are now entirely inappropriate and would have been hurtful to use. I have, however, after a lot of consideration and discussion with D, kept the term 'husband' in places. I would love there to be a less gendered term for what I understood my relationship to be at the points where I use it. I sincerely hope that this decision does not cause any hurt to any other members of the trans community. All views and experiences in this book are my own, and I am in no way attempting to represent the views or experiences of others.

I also hope that as our understanding of trans and non-binary lives and the issues that surround them evolve, so will our language. For now, I have done my best to honour both my story and my family in terms that get as close as possible to the experiences I am sharing with you.

PROLOGUE

'*Today I sat on a bench facing the sea, the one where I waited for L to be born, and sobbed my heart out. I don't know if I will ever recover.*'

This is a note on my phone, written on 9 November 2017.

I forgot about it for a couple of years, but when I look at it now I can remember typing it as if it were yesterday. The seagulls squawked overhead and the sun dipped into the sea, melting slowly as it met the horizon. I had been sitting there so long my hands were too cold to type. I put my phone back into the pocket of my winter coat, checked the baby's hat and blanket were secure, and turned the buggy to face home.

The conversation seemed un-haveable. But we had to have it. The vacuum in which my husband had been living since we had returned home with our newborn was now unbearable. The silences, the sadness, the sense that while there was boundless love between us, something had come loose and was now unspooling irrevocably, was intolerable.

The baby was six months old. He was so small he couldn't yet sit up without my hand in the small of his back to support him. His head had just about stopped bobbing around uncontrollably if left to its own devices. Only a week or two before, he had outgrown his newborn rocking crib, the little wooden cradle which had sat first next to me, and then at the end of our bed. The new, larger cot had just arrived. We had decorated his bedroom next door, me constructing the cot while D hung the mobile of floating paper clouds. I felt an ache like scar tissue on a cold day when I realised the three of us would no longer sleep together. My eyes were wet with tears as I placed him gently on his pristine new bedding a few hours later: our beloved angel on a puff of cloud. As D and I walked back to our own bedroom, there was nowhere left to hide. A few days later, after my return from that sunset walk, I took a deep breath and pressed my fingernails into the palms of my hands.

'I think you need to have some therapy,' I heard my voice say.

'You keep changing things about your appearance instead of accepting who you are,' I continued. 'It's what's inside that matters, you must know that. You're wonderful, we both love you so much. I wish you could relax and enjoy that.'

My husband replied slowly and reluctantly – knowing in advance just how the axis of our family was about to tilt. 'Yes, I do need to see someone. But . . . it's not because I can't, but because I *have* finally accepted who I am.'

'What do you mean?' I asked, unsure if the news was good or bad.

'I mean that I have accepted that I am not *this*.' A hand gestured at the body I had lain next to each night for the last five years. 'I have accepted that this body doesn't represent who I am.'

I almost heard my world crack in two.

I sensed my peripheral vision going fuzzy. The last time I had felt this was in the moments before passing out in a queue shortly after donating blood. By the time I had realised that the monochrome fuzz meant I was about to faint, my body was already halfway to the floor. A half-second of blissful surrender: there was nothing more I could do. The next thing I knew, a kind lady in an M&S tabard was offering me a sip of water.

This time I didn't hit the floor, but the sense of blissful surrender was the same. I felt myself falling, and I knew that there was nothing I could do about it. After so long, so many unasked and unanswered questions, and so much sadness, I knew in that instant that my husband was finally admitting to the need to transition.

It wasn't just this final revelation that tipped me off balance. It represented the latest in a series of destabilising experiences which had slammed into me like waves over the course of the last couple of years. In another life, this last piece of news might have destroyed me. I knew that many of those around me feared it still might.

The cumulative effect of medical misadventure, sexual assault and early motherhood in a marriage which felt inexplicably fractured, had left me spat out on the shore, unable to tell what was my body being churned through the water and what was the shingle moving away beneath me.

This bizarre succession of events had been so unexpected, and so intense, it left me reassessing essential truths not just about myself, but about what it is to be a woman, and what it is to live in a woman's body. As I watch my fingers type these words I cannot believe these hands belong to me. And that I survived. Not just that I survived, but that this strange and lonely period opened up the world, opened up my outlook and opened up my understanding of what beautiful variety we are all capable of.

1

This was not where my love story was supposed to end up. When D had appeared at my door six years earlier, drenched by a walk from the station in a seaside rainstorm and confessing, 'I love you', I felt my world expand, turn from black-and-white to technicolour, and sparkle in ways I had not known were possible. We had been close friends for some time, and now we were a couple. I always resisted the idea of a romance making me feel 'complete', but this time life simply felt *right.* D – with love, humour and boundless empathy – had the power to make my life seem as if it was being lived entirely in Portrait Mode: I was just a little sharper, a little better, a little more me. And everything else was a little blurry, a little less imposing than it used to be. As we moved seamlessly from couple to engaged couple, I never doubted that it would continue for ever.

D supported me as I wrote *Running Like A Girl*, the book which changed my life. After fifteen years of despair at the thought of physical exercise and a general sense of dissociation from my own body, discovering running – and then writing about it – had shown me a sense of self I had not dreamed possible. I, the one who had thought that the London Marathon would leave me with nothing more painful than a case of terminal eye roll, was training for my fourth when I met D. And each adventure filled me with greater grit and confidence than I had imagined possible. For so long I had taken for granted that there was some sort of barrier against me taking up and enjoying sport, and now it had turned out that it was entirely self-imposed. Sharing these revelations in print had only made the experiences all the sweeter.

It did not escape my notice that I finally let love in once I had found a physical way to respect the body I had been trying to wriggle away from for decades. D was on the end of the phone as I ran a marathon around San Francisco. D was waiting for me when I finished my final London Marathon. D was in the sea beside me when I took that first swimming lesson which became the opening scene for my next book, *Leap In.*

For years my family had longed for me to settle down with someone. Perhaps that isn't fair; what I suspect they truly wanted was for me to be loved by a partner as much as they loved me. And with D they saw that finally happen. My wedding day was a perfect pearl of a day, one I'll never forget, much less regret. I was finally letting myself believe that proper, official romance could be real.

And it was! I loved my new life. I enjoyed the new pace of living with someone, texting each other at the end of the day to check if we needed to bring anything home for dinner, having company during what had been the lonelier dips – the weekends or long January nights in – and laughing. *So* much laughing. Laughing like a drain at the silliest things, as a ludicrous but intimate language of nicknames and in-jokes began to coil itself around our day-to-day life and communications. I loved it all.

As the pain of miscarriage and the slow encroachment of fertility issues made their way first to our doorstep and into our home, we remained close, communicative, attentive to one another. D was ever supportive, ever understanding, ever kind. We were clear-sighted about the impact that fertility treatment might have on our marriage, and we were both keen to keep our cocoon of love untainted by it. Time spent with D – someone who had studied film and then worked in politics – was enriching on both a creative and an intellectual level. I felt truly cherished. But we knew that to take anything for granted was to place it at risk; we wanted to put in the hours and keep our marriage intact.

We had done our reading, we had consulted friends, we had talked to each other on long walks and late into the night. Our first round of IVF was a failure: the one embryo we created left my body almost immediately, and the impact of the drugs combined with a terrible bout of Norovirus left me physically and emotionally fragile for months. But we tried a second round, this time creating several embryos. The first resulted in an early failed pregnancy, and as the winter of 2015 turned to spring and then summer, we tried embryo after embryo, only to have my body fail to hold on to any of them. Neither of us wanted the other to feel pressured to keep trying for a baby if one of us felt defeated by the endeavour, but nor did we want to give up without affording ourselves the best possible chance of parenthood. Where to draw the line? Did we want to quit and end up a decade later thinking it hadn't been *that* hard, couldn't we have just gone on a *little* longer? Or did we want to stop wasting time pursuing an impossible dream and just enjoy our lives? When I wrote the final chapters of *Leap In*, I had all but lost hope. We had one embryo left, frozen at the fertility clinic, but I was not sure if we'd ever have the courage to use it – and potentially face the heartache all over again.

Two years after our wedding, and a little over a year after we had jumped through all the required admin and testing hoops and had begun the actual IVF treatment, we went on holiday to Portugal. A few days in Lisbon and a few days on the coast just outside Sintra. We ate seafood, lazed by the pool, we tried (and largely failed) to avoid rolling news as the Brexit vote came in and our country began its stumble into chaos. We came home and had the biggest argument of our marriage; a thundercloud of unspoken tension about anything and everything finally burst. Bottled-up anxieties about parenthood, politics, gender, ambition and where we wanted our joint future to head. We talked it through. We realised how close we had come to letting the process do to us what it had done to so many other couples, and we unearthed the fact that neither of us was ready yet to give up on the dream of having a child. Within a week we were closer to one another than ever before.

My body was exhausted by the drugs, my mind frazzled by living a constant half-life of plans unmade, dreams unrealised, and a relationship starting to buckle under the pressure. I wanted to move forward in a world unclouded by 'just in case'. If I wasn't going to surrender freedom to children, I didn't want it taken by IVF, and nor did D. We started to make plans for a life without children, looking at ways we could volunteer, at projects we could be a constructive part of, at people who might provide hope and a sense of optimism about a different future.

We began the process of accepting that parenthood, no matter how longed for, might not be for us after all.

We had never been an entirely conventional couple. Neither of us had ever felt quite comfortable with the idea of marriage as a goal; we both bristled at the borders of gender stereotypes in work and in life. I wanted women – myself included – to be liberated enough to be as strong and powerful as they wanted, without being tethered to ragged old notions of femininity meaning only slenderness and grace. Anatomy is not destiny, I would tell anyone who would listen, even louder as I felt the bindweed of infertility threaten to choke my status as a 'proper' woman. I wanted us to cheer at the football, sweat in the gym and feel free in a swimsuit. Meanwhile D bucked against equally tatty old suppositions about masculinity, with their required cheering at the football, aggression in the gym and admiration for women in swimwear. D wore a largely androgynous wardrobe, with as many skinny jeans as chinos, as many bias-cut tops as plain white T-shirts, and even occasionally painted nails. I was thrilled to have left behind the thick cotton of the rugby shirts I spent my twenties trying to escape. And D was far, far better at housework than me. I was the only woman I knew who had not cleaned her own kitchen since my wedding. Sure, I did all the cooking (because it was a passion), but perhaps this was finally the sort of gender equality I had longed for. Maybe this new path – without children – would be the one where our time and love would be best spent.

But first, that final embryo. After much discussion, we concluded that no matter how much pain the process had caused us, we simply could not leave one embryo, frozen, a mile down the road in the fertility clinic and expect to move on. We had to try everything. So we took a couple of months off treatment and then gave that final embryo a go.

To distract ourselves from the torment of the two-week wait before I could take a pregnancy test, we spent a week in Italy. I ate pasta, I swam in a pool overlooking the Umbrian hills where my family had holidayed for twenty years, and I visited the church where my sister had been married nine years earlier. As we flew home, I felt resigned to whatever the outcome might be. At peace, even.

We had given it our best shot. We had begun the whole IVF process optimistic, aware of our good fortune to have been referred for NHS treatment when so many other postcodes would not have deemed us eligible. I had worked hard on maintaining a positive state of mind, despite the setbacks and the physical struggle. I had started writing my new book, *Leap In,* with plans to swim from Alcatraz to San Francisco, to try to cross the Dardanelles, and beyond. My laptop hummed with tabs open and escapades half-organised, until my body ceased to be the crucible of self-esteem that I had come to rely on ever since I'd learned to run. Instead, I felt its tug keeping me close to home, to my love. I kept swimming – but locally. For an entire winter. Day after day, week after week, as the temperature dropped, I learned that warm acceptance of my physical self did not have to come from hours of training, sponsored swims and daring athletic feats, but that the small consistencies of turning up at the shore, determined to keep going, could be a salve to the soul too. I had fought to maintain this joy in my life, and was proud that I had kept moving when my body continued to fail me. Throughout it all, D had been there. At the water's edge with a towel and coffee. As the surgeons wheeled me out of the egg-collection procedures. As I struggled to write about such painful, turbulent times.

My time in the ocean had taught me that we can't always fight nature. Sometimes, we must accept what fate has assigned us. And as I recognised the dull ache of period pains setting in while we waited for our flight home, I let myself accept that, after everything, this reach for parenthood was an endeavour which had failed.

The flight was exceptionally beautiful. Dusk over Rome was followed by a perfect view of Nice, then Paris, the Eiffel Tower in all its glittering glory. Finally, the shoreline of Brighton unfurled below. Imagine, I thought to myself: the baby would have visited Rome, Paris and Brighton all in one night, before it was even born. When I undressed before bed, my knickers were stained by a streak of bright red. I put a pad in, and told D.

'I'm so sorry,' I howled into the same shoulder that had absorbed so many of my tears by then.

'Me too,' came the reply.

We held each other, repeating all the things we had told each other earlier that summer. All the promises made about a different, just as enriching, life without children. After all, we whispered in the dark, we still had each other.

I fell asleep, braced for pain. For the pain of a period which never came.

The next morning the pad was untouched by blood, and a few days later a blue line was unmistakable on the cheap own-brand pregnancy test I took. There was no doubting this line, it was all but pulsating with life. I indulged in a packet of the posh tests I had long ago stopped daring to buy, and did one a day for a week before summoning the courage to ring the midwife. It had been implantation pain I had experienced on the plane home. The embryo had taken: I was pregnant.

Those first few weeks of the pregnancy were as terrifying as they were wonderful. We told no one, and I rolled through the days, reeling and retching as if on board a boat. Something was undeniably happening to me, but the IVF had left me mistrustful of what was real, what was chemical, and what was imagined. How, just as I had finally reconciled myself to a future without children, was I expected to navigate this calmly?

My publishers wanted to discuss plans for *Leap In.* There was talk of publication in January, icy cold photo shoots in remote lakes and intrepid races to train for as promotional events. I knew I could not share such precious news with anyone else but my sister and a couple of very close friends until I knew the baby was safe. But how could I know the baby was safe?

The NHS did not have space for us to have a standard twelve-week scan. We would have to wait until fourteen weeks into the pregnancy, and I knew that the basic blood tests they would give me wouldn't be enough to determine whether the embryo might have any chromosomal disorders. I researched Edwards and Patau syndromes endlessly, checking details again and again, obsessing over the fact that I had just turned forty, as well as the 'artificial' nature of the embryo's conception. I knew none of this would help, but felt consumed by a sort of sadness. Each passing day seemed less like one closer to that magical twelve-week threshold when the most dangerous early trimester is over, and more like another day of being pregnant I would have to grieve for when the whole endeavour inevitably ended in disaster. The despondency was overwhelming: I felt haunted by the miscarriage I had had the previous autumn, convinced that the all-consuming heartache would return before too long.

D made valiant attempts to cheer me up and keep me calm. But consistent reminders that 'we've come this far, hold on to how exciting that is', only seemed to pile on the pressure. My sister echoed D's feelings, reminding me how important it was to stay positive, to keep letting that little embryo know how wanted it was. Just try and relax, she repeated. But still my mind churned with doubt – maybe that little embryo was wanted, but did it want to stay with me?

Thoughts of having an amniocentesis test, the prospect of the huge needle plunged into my uterus to collect amniotic fluid, were terrifying. And so were the statistics around its side effects. Having the test meant a very real chance of miscarriage, and taking that gamble in order for me to feel at ease, rather than for the good of the baby, was out of the question. Adding further risk to an already delicate situation was equally unpalatable. So we decided to pay for the new 'Harmony test', a privately available DNA test which looks at the blood of both mother and foetus, determining both the sex and the possibility of any chromosomal disorders with 99.9 per cent certainty.

We did not care about the sex, having long known that we would elect not to be told, nor were we put off by the potential challenges of bringing up a baby with Down's syndrome. But I was increasingly desperate to know whether the foetus might have the kind of chromosomal disorder which would mean it wouldn't survive beyond a day or two. I was quite sure that I could not carry a foetus to term, knowing that it wouldn't live. A quick scan, a blood test which would then be sent to a lab for testing, and a tap of the credit card was all it would take to find out via the Harmony test. The cost made me nauseous but then so did everything by that point. What could go wrong with a pinprick?

The day of the test I had a cup of tea with a friend who happened to be a mother of five. I confessed to her that my jitteriness was because of my pregnancy. She was thrilled, but her head sank into her hands when she heard of our decision to take the test.

'You've opened the gates!' she told me in despair. 'It will never end!'

'I just want to know that the baby is safe.'

'You can't *ever* know. The minute you know this, you will move straight on to the birth. Then the minute the baby's out you'll be worrying about cot death. As soon as you're clear of that you'll be panicking about them eating things from the floor, then they'll be able to bang their head when they start to move. Then it will be roads, then bikes, then they'll be going out without you and then they might take drugs or catch a flight without telling you and you'll lie awake all night worrying about that.'

I stared blankly.

'Oh God, parenthood is so awful. But it's all so exciting!'

How right she was.

That evening we caught the train to a small private clinic a long way outside of the city to have my bloods taken and for the accompanying scan. The sonographer's equipment was state of the art – it felt more like being in a recording artist's studio than a medical clinic. When the sound of the baby's heartbeat hit the enormous speakers, accompanied by vivid flickers on the giant wall-mounted screen, both D and I welled up at the sheer vitality of it. I felt a squeeze of my hand. 'You see?' it seemed to be telling me, as D's eyes never left the screen.

The room throbbed as we listened in surround-sound, watching the gentle swirl and swoop of the embryo inside me. I was so used to having blood tests by this point that I barely even noticed the samples being taken. Two, the sonographer told me – one to test and one extra just in case. You never know. We carried on chatting as the vials of blood were packaged up, the cardboard box prepared for mailing and the prepaid, barcoded label unpeeled and smoothed across the front of the packet. It was done. Soon, we would know.

A week later, the sonographer rang to say that one of the tests had come back unclear, so the lab was going to retest with the spare vial. I was frustrated that the tests I had paid for in order to get a speedy result were now going to be delayed, but understood that clarity was key. So we waited a few more days.

Late on Thursday afternoon, an hour or so before D was due home, the sonographer rang again.

'I'm just calling to double-check that you used a donor egg,' came the casual enquiry.

'No, I most definitely didn't,' I replied.

'Oh. It does say on your form that you used your own egg, but . . .'

'It was my egg. There is no way that getting those eggs out is something I would forget.'

'Weird . . .'

Weird.

It's rarely a word I relish hearing about myself. I'm not a pop star or an avant-garde artist. I don't particularly want to stand out. And hearing it from a medical professional? No, thank you.

I paused. Would there be any elaboration from this sonographer, who seemed so flummoxed by the results?

'Hmm, well, I don't know what that means.'

I sensed a shrug.

I said nothing. I felt the baby flick-flack inside me. Or was it just terror?

'I don't understand what you're telling me.' Nausea welled.

'Well, these tests have come back and they are saying that you don't seem to share DNA with the baby.'

My mind was starting to lurch, an unsteady passenger in a conversation that was reeling out of control.

'How can I not?'

'Yes, like I said, it *is* weird.'

'So the baby is . . . not mine?'

The slow realisation of what she was saying turned into a surge of horror.

'You're absolutely sure it wasn't a donor egg?'

'Of course I'm sure. I don't even know how to get a donor egg. I am absolutely sure they were mine.'

Flashes of the ceiling of the fertility clinic as I was wheeled into surgery, waiting for the anaesthetic to kick in before they repeatedly stuck the needle up my vagina to extract every single egg I had so painstakingly grown after weeks of injecting myself with hormones. Flashes of myself curled up in bed after the procedure, my abdomen cramping where the needle had pierced my ovaries. D bringing me dinner, smoothing the duvet around me as I rested, barely daring to make eye contact in case my body somehow let us down again. Flashes of me being called the next day, putting us immediately on speaker-phone, and the embryologist talking us through the quality and potential of each individual egg and the embryos they had become.

'OK, well, sometimes people lie.'

'Why would I lie? You know our history. I have had egg collection twice, and also gone through a failed pregnancy. This was our last embryo, our last chance.'

'Women can get ashamed if they have bad eggs. They go abroad and buy them, then say that they were theirs.'

'But mine were fine the second time. We made several embryos. I didn't *lie*! I'm not ashamed.'

How was the shame of strangers, their clandestine European egg-buying trips, relevant to me, now?

'Well, you need to telephone the clinic which treated you and check that they transferred the correct embryo to you.'

I was told I would receive a callback shortly. When our conversation ended I sat, still holding the telephone, as the possibilities which had just been thrown at me suddenly started to sink in.

If the embryo did not share any DNA with me, then whose was it? *Who* was it? Was it someone else's baby, a simple switch of embryos, an update on the switched-at-birth staple of soap operas? If so, where was our embryo? Our last precious embryo. Was it still in storage, frozen, waiting a mile away at the fertility clinic, or was it inside someone else? Had it already been born, during the time we had spent trying the other embryos? Was my baby shrieking and gasping on its first day alive while I had been eating linguine in Italy three months ago? Or had it been discarded? Labelled as another couple's embryo, then dismissed as unnecessary when another of their attempts had proved successful?

And what if a mistake had been made earlier, at the point of fertilising the egg? Was I carrying another woman's embryo, but one which had been made with D? Or was another woman carrying my embryo, fertilised by someone else's sperm? And in which of these cases would I keep the baby?

For so long I had been filled with a sense that it wasn't worth trying to bond with this embryo, that I should somehow keep it at an emotional arm's length. The countless nights I had spent awake, tormenting myself for 'making up worries'. The times my mother and sister had asked me when I would be happy about my news, instead of obsessing over what might go wrong. *I had been right all along*, I said to myself.

I telephoned D, who came home from work immediately. I called the fertility clinic, and left a panicked voicemail. We paced the flat, repeating random sentences and confused questions like cartoon people who have received bad news, only we had no idea how bad the news was, or what could be done about it. We paced some more, frantic, trying to work out what we had been told, me running through the conversation again and again, trying to establish what the salient facts actually were.

It was several hours before we heard back from the sonographer at the private clinic which had taken my sample. We were forwarded an email from the London laboratory that had processed the bloods, telling the private sonographer that there was '*the presence of an additional DNA source in them*'. The email also mentioned that *'repeat testing will not generate a result'* because they had tested both vials. They were telling us that it was not a laboratory mistake, because they had run the tests twice, with the same result.

I left a second, increasingly desperate voicemail on the fertility clinic's out-of-hours number, begging for someone to call us back. Fears about who was growing inside me were blossoming with each passing minute. No one but me seemed to be concerned about this potential impostor. D had quite rightly taken a very firm line that everything was going to be OK, that we simply needed the facts and we would work from there. Which was easier said than done.

I called the same friend I had seen only a few hours earlier and explained my panic. Luckily, she was someone who knew a lawyer, and mercifully that lawyer was decent enough to call us within an hour. By then, my search engine was overheating with the strange word combinations I had tried.

Wrong baby give back court case
Embryo swap case
IVF baby mistake

To my horror I discovered that there *had* been cases where women had been mistakenly impregnated with an embryo that was not genetically theirs. Cardiff, Ohio, Northern Ireland. The author Maggie O'Farrell had even written about it, the headline quoting a mother:

'*I love him to bits, but he's probably not mine.*'

However, these cases had thus far only been discovered post-birth. The Harmony test was a prenatal DNA test: it had not previously been possible to check and compare a foetus's DNA against the parents'. My heart juddered and my stomach constricted. Everything seemed to be becoming more confused. We were dealing with a situation without legal precedent: the UK law stated that a surrogate – anyone who gave birth to a baby but was not its biological parent – was its legal parent. But the government website had nothing about a situation in which you might have ended up an inadvertent surrogate – or indeed have your own embryo being carried by an inadvertent (and in this case unknowing) surrogate.

Once on the line, the lawyer exuded the sort of calm and confidence that only true experts possess. He repeated that we had to get the tests entirely redone, and that that had to happen as soon as possible. Until we had facts, we could not make any decisions. I don't remember a huge amount more about the conversation, except that my mobile phone sat on the coffee table, switched to speakerphone as we tried to take notes. When I look at those notes now, I don't recognise the handwriting as my own. Once the words 'no legal precedent' had been uttered, an internal buzz of terror seemed to overwhelm me. And by the look on D's face, the terror was not mine alone. No one knew the rules. No one understood the situation. No one had ever felt like this before.

That static buzz continued, growing to a screech of inner feedback every time I imagined my stomach growing with a baby I had not invited into me. We did our best to soothe each other before bed, to accept that there was nothing we could do that night, to make peace with the fact that any real sleep would be a lofty ambition. I had my first alcoholic drink for twelve weeks, letting myself almost inhale a small shot of single malt while I lay on the new sofa we had dared to buy as part of our nascent nesting. We held hands and watched an entire series of a property show which snooped around homes on the coast. House after house of sea views and deep blue diamond-sprinkled shots of the ocean.

My body was vibrating on a sort of invisible, molecular level. If a third person had walked into the room that evening they would not have noticed me breathing using only the top 20 per cent of my lungs, or felt the prickles of anxiety running across me like the wind catching damp skin after a swim. They would never even have known that I was pregnant. To an outsider I would have looked perfectly relaxed. And despite this hum of panic coursing through me, a steady drip of cortisol with every beat of my heart, a detached sort of calmness did, slowly, envelop me.

For so many weeks now, this little embryo, the one who stayed, had felt not like a blessed gift, a source of joy, a future human – but like grief, waiting for me. But now something else was happening: as we tried to relax, something strange was changing in my relationship with this little thing. My thoughts were still blossoming – questions, possibilities, scenarios leading one into the other with alarming speed. But somehow this was the point at which I felt myself connect with this embryo. For so long I had been willing it to stay but not willing to commit to it. I hadn't wanted to confront my joy, to embrace my relief, to celebrate our luck. I just wanted the pain to burst open so I could start to heal all over again.

Now, however, I saw the embryo as a being, as someone I needed to protect. Not just as a source of my own future joy but potentially a joy belonging to someone else. What if our baby was growing elsewhere – would I not want someone tending to it? So I had to do the same for this one, whoever it might be. By midnight I was eating a fistful of spinach straight from the fridge, worrying that that shot of whisky might have done some damage. It had suddenly become real for me.

We slept fitfully that night, barely ever slipping into more than a doze. I lay on my back, my breathing shallow, and nodded off for perhaps half an hour at a time. I thought I had known anxiety before – restless sleep, tangled sheets, sweaty forehead – but this was a world of constant alertness, adrenaline relentlessly pumping through my system. I had to keep reminding myself to breathe, focusing on the overhead lamp I had barely noticed in three years of living in that flat, my hand resting on my flat stomach, hoping some oxygen would make it down there past the thick clouds of cortisol gathering in me like cholesterol in a smoker's arteries. I felt sure my mind was audible, thrumming like a fridge freezer. By 4 a.m. I had stopped trying not to think, and let myself wander freely through the interminable variety of outcomes my imagination was determined to sling at me.

Would I return the baby if it wasn't ours or mine? Yes, I felt sure I would. I had to keep it safe and well for whoever's it was. Could I co-parent with D if it was D's but not mine? Yes, I was sure I could. This was no longer about ego or my wishes – those things were long gone. Scenario after scenario scrolled past, a jerking montage I was not seeing through my own eyes but from above, shot by a drone swooping gently overhead, watching how each horrific possibility could play out. Here I was in a conference room, a lawyer's office, a court, handing over the baby to its rightful parents. I went through the logistics, inconsequential details preoccupying me for what seemed like hours at a time. What would I need to wear to make the newborn calm and secure? Would a comforting outfit be suitable for such a formal event? Did I already have clothes that I would be happy to throw away afterwards, not wanting to be reminded of that day, or would I buy something new especially for the occasion? What could such an outfit be?

As each scene flashed by – me, discovering that the baby was D's but not mine; me, drinking a protein shake to look after this stranger's baby; me, somehow having kept the baby but looking noticeably not like its parent – the distance between myself and my own body grew a little. I saw myself set apart from the reality I was experiencing. My present and particularly my future were too terrifying. I could see them only as others might: the baby's 'real' parents, the baby, the doctors and lawyers who would end up trying to unravel this.

I became so mistrustful that this experience was actually mine, that it was me going through this and not an actress playing me while I watched from afar, that the next morning I decided I should record everything that went on. If I wasn't really there, I had to keep a note of everything for when I returned. The situation needed documenting, day by day, and if things could go this wrong, I would need to keep a sharp eye out from now on.

Very early the next morning we were called by the fertility clinic which had performed the embryo transfer and invited in for a meeting in a couple of hours' time. We were exhausted and shaky after that strange night, but made each other breakfast, tried to comfort each other about what lay ahead for the rest of the day, and began the same walk to the clinic that we thought we had left behind us a couple of months ago. Hand in hand, retreading our steps into a future that seemed more fraught than anything else we had thus far imagined as we had headed to West Hove and the team we thought we would never see again.

When we arrived we quickly saw that the staff at the clinic felt no less fraught. It was clear that some of them had been up for hours, and it seemed that one or two had been crying. A huge pile of paperwork was on the consultant's desk, and the full team of almost everyone who had treated us, from nurses to embryologists, was in the room. I felt enormous relief that at last we were being taken seriously – and a stab of fear that they deemed it to be so serious.

The first thing the team did was to explain that they had been reluctant to call us back until they had thoroughly researched our treatment records; they only dealt with facts, not suppositions. Then the staff explained that they had retrieved not only the records for every time we were in the building, for each of the embryos we had created and their individual barcodes, but also for every other patient who had been treated in the clinic on any of the same days as us. The first glimmer of hope we felt was at the news that no embryos created on the same days as ours had been destroyed. Each was accounted for. Some of those embryos had now grown into babies and been born, some had not survived, but none were missing.

When we started treatment, we had been issued with credit card-sized photo IDs with an individual barcode, which were swiped at every stage. I rarely thought about it at the time, I was so used to chip-and-pin payments, library photocopying cards and swiping to enter hotel rooms on book tours. But it turned out our every movement was tracked while we were in treatment, as the two-foot-high stack of paperwork testified. Things had clearly moved on since the cases I had Googled. But had they moved on far enough? It was of course wonderful news that none of our embryos had been lost, but if I did not share DNA with the embryo, then who was in me?

The team from the clinic passed my phone around between them, reading and rereading the email from the sonographer, scrolling for an explanation that made sense. They were baffled as to what the term '*the presence of an additional DNA source*' could mean, and similarly perplexed by the confident assertion that '*repeat testing will not generate a result*'. Of course the tests needed to be redone. How could they not be?

After the very early start, and the several hours they had evidently spent checking data, the team were pretty sure that there were only two realistic explanations: a lab mistake, or a rare condition called mosaicism. It was explained to us that mosaicism is a DNA condition in which it is possible to be composed of cells of two genetically different types. This could have serious chromosomal implications for a child, so we would need to find out more as soon as possible. Added to this was the fact that we had still not had any results for the barrage of chromosome disorders that the Harmony test was actually supposed to have checked for. And of course it was hard to ignore the possibility that, until full repeat tests were carried out, there was still a small chance the baby was not mine at all.

As we sat in the consulting room, the director of the clinic telephoned a contact of hers at a renowned Harley Street practice. She was sending us to the internationally acclaimed specialist Professor Kypros Nicolaides. We listened as she painstakingly explained to his assistant that we needed to be seen as soon as possible, and that yes, we did need both paternity and maternity tests. Again I watched my own body language, as though from above, as my hand twitched at the mention of my urgent need for a maternity test. In order to unravel the mysteries of my DNA and that of my embryo I would have to have a procedure almost identical to the very test I had paid to avoid: a Chorionic Villus Sampling or CVS test. Differing from an amniocentesis because it takes a sample of the placental tissue rather than the amniotic fluid, it would still involve a 7.5cm needle being inserted through my belly in order to retrieve the necessary cells. And it would carry an even higher risk of miscarriage: 1 per cent. But we all agreed that it was the only option. An appointment was made, and we had only the weekend to get through.

Only the weekend.

'Just try and stay relaxed.' Again.

There was no possible way to relax. At best we could distract ourselves. We went shopping in Brighton and allowed ourselves to buy a first item of clothing for whoever it was who was living with us. To indulge in baby clothes seemed too wildly optimistic, so we bought a T-shirt for a one-year-old covered in cats wearing spacesuits. '*Catstronauts!*' it declared cheerily. Neither of us had any interest in either cats or space, but its optimism was the only thing that had made us smile in forty-eight hours. Perhaps a nephew could wear it, if it never found an owner in our home.

We had lunch in our local bookshop and spent hours browsing any topic that might hold our attention for more than eighty seconds. We came away with a book on Brutal London, complete with small cut-out Brutalist buildings to make. We spent the rest of the afternoon carefully pressing along the perforations and folding the stiff paper to create a tiny Barbican, a tiny Royal Festival Hall, a tiny Trellick Tower. Nothing looks less like baby paraphernalia than a Brutalist building rendered paper-doll size. But nothing felt less like pregnancy than waiting to be pierced in the belly to discover if I was the baby's mother.

Eventually Monday came, and we made our way to Marylebone shortly after the weekday rush hour had subsided. Professor Nicolaides's clinic was like no other medical environment I have ever been in. It seemed more like an art gallery, its waiting area filled with huge sculptures alongside indecently low designer leather sofas. The receptionist had the sort of polished glamour I would expect in an aesthetician's consulting room. The hush of money and the discretion it affords washed over us. Until we explained who we were and who had sent us.

'Ah yes, you're here for a paternity test' might for some be the very nadir of shame. I bettered it with a sheepish 'and maternity test' and observed the subtle whisper of confusion as eyes flickered across the screen.

We sat and waited, unsure if we were welcome to look at the design magazines, quietly missing our tiny Brutalist city on the bookcase at home. We were ushered into separate rooms for blood tests, then I was given a scan which lasted over an hour. The sonographer looked like a Scandinavian supermodel, and had the effortless charm and confidence that can surely only be acquired by knowing you work in the best clinic in London.

We watched the foetus for what seemed like for ever as it spun and swam, its hands up by its ears like a miniature sunbather, its huge reptilian feet swooshing as it played in its fluid home. We were allowed to video it, and were given endless screengrabs to take home. There was no sign that it was anything but perfectly healthy. We knew that the sonographer knew its sex but we had continued to ask not to be told. *Please, let us have one happy surprise. Let one unknown be a choice.* When I look at the photograph I took of my hand holding one of the small images printed off for us, I see that my fingernails were varnished an immaculate navy blue. I have no recollection of painting them.

Eventually, Professor Nicolaides himself arrived. Like a master showman, he seemed to know on sight what his audience needed. He saw in us two people who needed not mere reassurance but epic distraction.

'So! The scandalous couple with the mysterious baby!' he declared in his thick Cypriot accent, his arms raised in welcome as we stepped into his consulting room. He shook our hands warmly, clasping my cold, nervous fingers between his two huge palms. I was invited to sit up on a bed, while D sat on an expensive-looking chair beside me.

'I am quite sure I know what happened,' Professor Nicolaides announced. His confidence but also his determination to relax us beamed from him as he swung around on his chair, tapping a couple of keys on his computer and then kicking his legs back and forth as he whizzed round from screen to us and back.

'The lab technician, they had a curry.' He grinned impishly. 'It was a bad curry. They are doing your results the next day, suddenly they have to run to the bathroom, they come back and they write up the right results in the wrong document, the wrong column, the wrong form, whatever. We all say it never happens . . . but it happens.'

'But they said they tested both vials of my blood,' I protested. 'They said a retest won't matter.'

'Of course they'll say that, they made a mistake and they don't want to get found out. Not everyone is a professional. Not everyone has experience. But *we* can sort this out. We must.'

He shrugged and smiled. At last someone was saying out loud what I had been longing to hear: *You are not mad. You are not making a fuss. You are not being unreasonable to want to know what is happening in your body.*

He moved on quickly, barely letting up on his stream of conversation. He explained that he had checked the scans we'd just had and everything looked OK. We laughed at the enormous size of the baby's feet. Each bit of banter was a tiny pinprick of hope, but nothing he said really relaxed me because I knew what was coming next.

IVF changed my relationship with needles. Once I began to associate those slim metal tips with life, and hope, I had become a relaxed expert at injecting myself, able to do it in restaurant lavatories, on fast-moving trains and even when a nephew came barrelling unexpectedly into my sister's bathroom. But back then I had been injecting myself. And those needles were whisper thin.

The needle for the CVS was significantly larger. And it had to go deep into me, to meet whoever was in there, taking fluid from the placenta. And it was right there, prepared and lying on a steel dish. It was just that I hadn't seen it yet.

While we were talking, Professor Nicolaides was physically manoeuvring me onto the bed, patting the headrest to enourage me to sit back, then tipping the bed so that I was lying flat, chatting all the while. He nodded to me to raise my top and I did it silently, while the three of us maintained our lighthearted patter. Still I said nothing as a nurse leaned in and wiped an area on my belly with antiseptic. We carried on joking about the wonders of his scanning equipment and I lifted a hand to gesticulate. As I did, he caught it mid-air. I did not understand what was happening, but quickly, he lifted my other hand to be part of that same grip. Still talking, he had both of my hands secured. And then, with a sleight of hand I will never forget, the needle was in me. I felt the puncture as if I'd been shot.

In a second it was over.

My arms would doubtlessly have flung up in shock if they had not been so neatly clasped out of harm's way. The needle was whipped out before I had finished gasping. The pain had immediately flowered, but already it was fading. Already, I was recovering. Now we had only to rest and wait for the results.

I went to the bathroom where I lifted my top, gazed down at the site of the puncture and stroked myself, willing whoever was in there to stay safe.

I'm sorry, I whispered, *we didn't mean to frighten you. And don't worry, we'll take care of you.*

I closed my eyes and prayed that the baby was mine.

It was only about a week before we had the results of the embryo's maternity and paternity tests, but it was six weeks before each of the further chromosome tests' results were relayed to us. We were telephoned as each result came in, a constant drip drip drip of news. Yes, the foetus you are carrying is definitely both yours and D's. Yes, your DNA is both entirely distinct from, and yet clearly related to, that of your foetus. Yes, the results are good regarding Edwards syndrome. Yes, the results are good regarding Patau syndrome. Yes, the results are good regarding Prader-Willi syndrome. And finally, no, there is no sign of mosaicism. You have a healthy embryo, with a 99.9 per cent chance of no chromosomal disorders. The only explanation for the mix-up was either lab or communication error.

The relief was enormous, particularly as by now terminating the pregnancy for any reason would have been hugely distressing for both of us. But also because we were finally able to talk openly about what we had been going through. Six weeks is a long time in what you know will be your only pregnancy. The combination of early pregnancy's dreamy haze, as well as the closed-down state of self-preservation I had unwittingly put myself into, means I can't remember a huge amount about day-to-day life at this point. As it became slowly apparent that our distress had been caused by nothing more than someone, somewhere's, lack of professionalism or accountability, I started to miss what those weeks should have been, even as I was living them.

When any one of us tries to get pregnant, we daydream about the congratulations, the hugs, the emotional scenes as you tell loved ones. We daydream about the first time your hand cradles the beginnings of a bump. We daydream about telling ourselves, *yes, it's happening. It's more than a blue line now – we're doing this.* But all those early daydreams were lost to us, or at least untouchable beneath all the anxiety. Occasionally I would try to get a little purchase on one of them, only to feel it slide out of my grasp, slippery with fears and unanswered questions.

During that six-week wait for the full results, colleagues had been told the bare facts in formal tones by my agent as work was suddenly cancelled. Jolly texts saying everything was fine were sent to family members while the telephone went unanswered. My hand didn't dare cradle any hint of a bump, lest I became too close to someone whose hand I would eventually be waving goodbye to.

Each week my pregnancy app would announce that the foetus was now the size of a raspberry, a Greek olive, a plum. Each week the app described the emergence of eyelashes, the development of fingernails and genitalia, and I would whisper to each organ, each eyelash, each fingernail. *Be mine. Stay safe. We'll make it.*

With each phone call from Professor Nicolaides's team, I felt closer to the baby. It wasn't just the certainty that this baby was ours, the relief that I wasn't steeling myself for another goodbye. It was a sense that this little being and I had endured something *together*. We hadn't let each other down, we hadn't given up on each other, we had made it through.

D had been a peerless support, with me throughout. But D's body had gone untouched. The baby and I had felt that thick slosh of adrenaline as we were told we might not belong together, we had felt the gunshot of that needle entering us, and we had lain together at night, awake at the same times, at peace at the same times, waiting. Waiting to be told. It was this shared experience which at last let me exhale, and trust that this pregnancy might be something more than just tomorrow's grief.

To this day, Professor Nicolaides's explanation of what had happened seems to be the most plausible one. The private sonographer never apologised, nor did they offer any further explanation. Perhaps they were just too far out of their depth, having to deliver any news beyond a healthy heartbeat. They wrote back to our letter of complaint saying that they had provided us with excellent care, and at that point I was advised by the consultant looking after us at the hospital where I would give birth to cease contact, for the sake of my blood pressure.

At last, after those long weeks, we were able to celebrate. The pregnancy could be discussed with joy in our voices, rather than in barked bullet points of information. Finally, we were able to imagine the baby actually existing outside me. But this in turn left me feeling as if my body was not my own, but a mere theatre for the drama we had just endured.

Achieving a pregnant state in itself already felt like something I had been a passive observer to. I had been unconscious as eggs were taken from me, sedated while one by one they were relocated once fertilised, and then had sat in countless doctors' consulting rooms being discussed as a problematic case, perhaps not even a mother.

We went away to Bath for the weekend, my maternity jeans at last clinging to the beginnings of my bump. We drank water from the Pump Rooms, we ordered endless room service and we slept properly in an enormous, luxurious bed. Don't think about legal action now, I was advised, enjoy the pregnancy. Enjoy the baby. Think about it in a few months. Months! I had months now to enjoy it all, I told myself.

2

The rest of the pregnancy itself was mostly simple. I was tired but felt well. I wrote an entire book, I enjoyed Christmas, I kept lists of potential baby names, possible swaddling blankets and babygros. I swam in the sea several times a week, I walked for miles around Dungeness on my birthday weekend with D, I enjoyed pregnancy Pilates, slowly creeping up the class until I was one of the largest bumps.

I even felt a complicated pride as my bump began to show, and more people commented on it. I *was* proud of it, but there was resentment there too. It wasn't an achievement to be proud of, it was luck. Fate and science had been kind to me, and I would have been no less proud of myself had that last embryo not worked. I felt validated by my pregnancy as much as I felt furious for a potential other me who might not have had the same luck. Would she have been seen as less of a woman, doing less womanly things? I thought of friends who had not succeeded, of readers I had started to hear from since the publication of *Leap In*, of those other faces I used to see in the fertility clinic's waiting room. We were all women; I was just a lucky one.

A few weeks before the baby was due I headed to London for lunch with my siblings to celebrate my sister's birthday. We had tapas in South London, sharing giggles about the impending birth, who we'd be meeting as a result and laughing at the volume of olive oil I managed to spill down my bump as I greedily lifted bread to my mouth. I even had a glass of Prosecco.

After lunch, my sister and I went back to hers and into her spare room where she had laid out baby blankets which had been knitted for us by some Italian family friends, a breast pump she had never got on with and some of the newborn clothes we had worn as infants which had been saved by my mother and then her. We folded everything into a couple of canvas bags, carefully trying to work out how much I could manage on what I had already decided would be my last train trip to London. Before leaving the house, my brother-in-law and I checked what time Crystal Palace would be playing, so that I could avoid boarding a train in South London just as a legion of emotional football fans were heading home. I was by this stage carrying my medical notes with me at all times, as my blood pressure was creeping up and consultants were starting to mutter quietly about a potential induction. I made sure to leave in good time, and sat exhausted, surrounded by soft family heirlooms as the train left the city behind.

A couple of stops later a clutch of men, probably about my age, boarded the train with the unsteady gait of those who have enjoyed an afternoon of drinking. They were smartly dressed in pointy lace-up shoes and mid-length navy raincoats. One of them went to sit down opposite me, the movement of the train as it pulled away leaving him swaying directly over my bump. I looked up anxiously, not sure if he was even capable of noticing how close he had come to knocking it. *Us.* He looked back at me, and slurred, 'Hello, darling.' As he said this, he stroked the back of my hand, which was resting on a blanket bag on my lap, with the backs of his own tattooed fingers. He was not saying hello. This was no proposition. He was not sexually attracted to me, let alone to the degree that he simply couldn't control himself: he was instead baffled that I had not responded with delight to his uninvited approach. And because I had had the temerity to respond publicly to his arrival with anxiety, he was now becoming riled. I didn't want to engage on any terms, as it was clear how intoxicated he was. Perhaps he hadn't even noticed my bump, swathed in winter clothes and coats as it was.

I looked down, knowing that my only safe option was to sit elsewhere. With a lurch as unsteady as his, I grabbed my bags and stood up to move. At nearly nine months pregnant I was an unmissable obstacle in the aisle of the train carriage. My arse was by now almost as large as my bump. It could not be reached for in error, up and under a large jacket. Yet that is exactly what happened next. A hot male hand grabbed my behind as I passed the man's seat. I flinched, trying to shrug it off as I rocked with the momentum of the carriage to get away from him.

'What's your fucking problem?' the man muttered as I recoiled.

I bristled, aware that the rest of the now-busy carriage was listening. I was afraid to provoke him any further, knowing that I was on a conductor-less train. But I also wanted my fellow passengers to realise that I felt afraid.

'My fucking problem is your hand on my arse,' I said, at what I hoped was a volume audible to others but not likely to increase the level of threat. I walked through the glass doors to the first-class section at the very front of the train, as close as I could be to the driver's cabin. I put on my headphones and tried to breathe slowly. *Just stay calm. Just stay calm. Just stay calm.*

I didn't think I was about to be harmed any further. I was quite sure that a grabbed backside would not cause my baby any damage. And I was now safely out of the man's reach. But my mind was ablaze. A floodgate of adrenaline had been opened and my raging heart was pumping it faster and faster through every vein in my body. Blinded by panicked confusion at something so unexpected happening, my anxieties derailed – I worried about being fined for sitting in first class. So I tweeted the rail company.

'*I am sitting, alone, in first class on the train that just left ECR from platform 3 for Brighton. If any of your staff would like to challenge me on this it is because a passenger has just slapped my hand, then arse. I am 8 months pregnant and not keen to go back and photograph him but will do if you need me to. Hopefully your CCTV will have caught this.*'

I copied a link to the tweet and texted it to my husband, saying, '*This just happened, can you meet me at the station?*'

While I waited for a response, I heard the glass doors behind me slide open and shut again as three passengers entered. Three of the men's friends came and sat behind me. They discussed, loudly, what a liability he was, and how he needed to stop getting into trouble while drinking. One of these days he'll really upset someone, they agreed.

D called me back within a couple of minutes, asking if I was OK, and if the train company had seen my message.

'Let me know when they reply. I'm heading to the station now.'

'OK, I will, but we're getting to the section of the journey with no reception soon, so don't worry.'

'Of course I'm worried! That's sexual assault!'

'I KNOW it's sexual assault,' I snapped back, although at that point I really didn't. I was afraid and furious, but in the blinding heat of panic I had not stopped to think that is what had happened.

Yet as I said those words I heard the chatting of the three men behind come to an abrupt stop. I hurriedly ended the conversation with D, and returned my headphones to my ears.

The train company replied to my tweet, adding British Transport Police who said I should send them my mobile number if I needed them to call me. As I was typing out my reply I became aware of a man standing at my shoulder.

I removed one headphone and looked at him.

'What were you saying on the phone just then?'

'I was talking to my husband.'

'Well, what were you saying?'

'It doesn't matter, I'm fine.'

'My mate's not fine though.'

'I really don't want to talk about it.'

'Well, you were happy to shout about it back then in a carriage full of people.'

'Seriously, I just don't want to talk about it!' I replaced my headphone and stared out of the window to avoid eye contact. Dusk was falling fast, and the train was speeding through the South Downs. Soon we would be out of mobile reception. The man continued to talk.

'What you were saying back then was a lie.'

'It wasn't a lie. Please, can we just leave it?'

The man's two friends had swung their legs out so that the path to the glass doors and out of the carriage was blocked. There was nowhere for me to go.

'Seriously, everyone in that carriage saw what you did.'

'I. Don't. Want. To. Talk. About. It.'

'They're all back there calling you a liar, they know you are.'

'I am not lying.'

'Look, if you feel like you've been touched—'

'I don't feel like I've been touched. I *have* been touched. Twice.'

'Well, if that's what you feel happened to you—'

'It's not what I feel happened to me. It's what happened.' My voice was rising in panic. I know this because I was so afraid that I recorded this conversation on my phone's camera. I still have it, just a few squares along from those first scan photographs. I watched it again this morning. I couldn't hold the phone up to film properly so the shot is from my hand as I gesticulate: three pairs of smart lace-ups pointing into the aisle, and the top of my bump.

'Well, there was someone opposite who stood up straight away and said, "That didn't happen." And we don't know that person. But they've already come forward and said, "I'm happy to stick up for that guy." So given that, do you not think you've made a mistake?'

'I *know* I didn't make a mistake. I *know* what happened.'

And so it continued, three men blocking my path out of the carriage, telling me that what had just happened to my body had not. The train driver a door away, unable to help me. I could see no way out of the carriage without being touched again. I was shaking with fear, but trying to breathe deeply in the hope that I could at least prevent any harm to my unborn baby.

The recording I made is interrupted when a woman comes into the carriage to ask if I am OK. When I reply that no, I am not, I really, really am not, she ushers me out to sit with her and her partner in the adjacent carriage. Moments later, the man who assaulted me leaves that carriage to sit with his friends in first class at the front of the train.

British Transport Police took my tweet seriously and asked, via Twitter, if I needed help. I told them my situation and they arranged to have police at the station when I arrived home. I agreed to this, but was unprepared for the animal agitation of hearing sirens I knew I had summoned as the train pulled in, then the jittery wait in my seat until the man and his friends had left the train.

As they got off, they dropped and smashed the bottles of fizzy wine they had had with them, leaving the station concourse sticky with sweet alcohol. They staggered and swayed to the side of the station and out of view while my new friends took me directly to the waiting police and my husband who had run to meet me.

A jumble of conversation followed. Me trying to tell D what had happened, policemen talking to each other, station staff explaining where the men had exited the station. And then a woman and her family approached the group.

'Hi,' she smiled at us. 'I was on that train. And I saw everything that happened. If you need me as a witness I will be there.'

'You saw?' I asked, agog. How quickly I had let myself doubt my own judgement. Tiredness and an urgent desire to be alone, in bed, had already led to a whisper which was becoming a shout that perhaps I had imagined it after all. Perhaps I was overwrought. Perhaps I should just shut up and go home.

'Yes, I was with my family sitting behind you and we saw it all.'

'But his friends came and told me that everyone in the carriage was talking about how I had made it up . . .'

'That's not true. We saw. And we told them we saw.'

'Thank you,' I whispered, my knees by now almost giving out beneath me. 'Thank you so much for telling me that.'

One of the group of police stepped forward to take her details, and as she was led away, I mouthed thank you to her once more.

A day out in London by this stage in my pregnancy was a gargantuan effort anyway, but one involving a high-energy lunch, carrying large bags home and then half an hour of confrontation and a police escort had left me thinking that only the third understudy was available to play the role of me that evening. I was empty, exhausted, barely there.

The police took us to their car and we waited in the back seat while the man was found at the rear of the station, arrested and taken away in a police van. I was then asked if I would like to pursue the matter. My instinct was to say no. I just wanted everything and everyone to leave me in peace so I could unpack my baby blankets and watch a bit of telly.

'Is there anything to be gained by it? Really?' I asked the two officers in the front seats.

The woman in the passenger seat turned to me. When she saw what she must have recognised as hesitation on my face she said, 'It *was* a crime. You *can* pursue it.' It was only then that I considered it seriously.

'Really?'

'It depends how you see it. You are a reliable witness. You have a second witness. And those trains have CCTV. You have as good a chance as any of getting a conviction. But you're about to have a baby and you might not fancy having us lot calling you up for a few months.'

'Would I have to go to court?'

'Yes, but with a case like this, we are able to put in a request for things to be delayed so you can have a few months without having to think about it. You are, after all, a vulnerable witness.'

Vulnerable.

It took someone else to say it, in the very last month of my pregnancy, for me to realise how I had been feeling all this time: so very exposed. And yet . . . as I sat in the back of that police car, I knew that I had looked after myself as well as anyone could in that situation. I had a good support network. I was articulate. I was, despite my exhaustion, strong. Yes, I was vulnerable, but I was something more than that too. And I *had* something more than that. Although I didn't feel it in that instant, I am privileged. I am white, I am well spoken. I have many of the attributes that lawyers look for in a witness, and many of the attributes that mean I will always have an easier ride in the justice system than many others. So if I was not prepared to stand up and be counted how could

I expect anyone without my advantages and support network to do so?

'The other thing to remember is that if you pursue it, the case will show up in records. When governments look at what sorts of crimes are being reported and committed yours will show up. You will be part of a bigger picture, shaping how decisions are made for us and so on . . .'

'I get it,' I said quietly. 'I want it to count. I don't want it to have been for nothing. I'll do what you need.'

3

There is talk of the 'animal self' that takes over when birth is imminent, or when a woman is in labour. It is discussed in reverent tones at birthing classes – the friend who has had the most Prosecco at the baby shower often brings it up – and birthing blogs love to reassure their readers that it's perfectly natural, nothing to fear or feel shame about. A 'you' emerges who you had never imagined existed, making decisions entirely on instinct, guttural primeval howls emerging as contractions kick in, volcanic emotions startling partners and parents alike.

I had done my hypno-birthing classes, had bought my battery-operated fairy lights and made my birthing playlist. I had stopped short of writing out my affirmations with a sparkly rollerball pen on some pretty pastel paper – but only just. Yes, I was ready to retreat into my cave and experience the journey taken by millennia of women as they cross the threshold into that most sanctified of clubs: motherhood. Yet my birth story saw me as passive as a back-seat traveller: it was less a mystical journey, more me having my passport stamped at customs. Hours of waiting, the lower-back ache ever increasing, then BAM! – over to the other side.

For years I had heard the term 'highbloodpressure' as one word without really considering its component parts. I suppose I knew what it meant, but it had never concerned me, so I had never given it more than a passing moment's thought. Around the time of the assault on the train, mine had started to rise. Now, the literal pressure of my blood pumping through my body was high. And it felt high. In fact, it was starting to feel grotesque.

Prick me, and I will burst.

Now, obstetric consultants were suggesting that an induction would be advised, and imminently. I was by this point so resigned to being a passenger on whatever journey my body was about to take that I did not fight the decision when it was put to me – despite the cries of friends who told me to wait, to hold my nerve. Had I not been holding my nerve long enough by now? Could I not let someone else take just one decision for me?

A week before my son was officially due, on a crisp and clear morning at the seaside, I waddled to the maternity ward, lifted my legs akimbo yet again, and let a midwife insert the induction drugs up and into my vagina. Then I lay back on my NHS regulation pillows and awaited the ride. The awful thing about induction, they all told me, is that it makes things happen so artificially fast. *Ride, I am ready*, I thought as I tried to breathe slowly.

Twenty-four hours later, I was still on the ward, untroubled by so much as a whisper of a contraction. Yes, my back ached, but that had been going on for six months. D had headed home for the night. 'Get some sleep! You'll need it tomorrow when the fun begins!'

I was alone, bored, and tired of the woman one curtain away who was dealing with her alarmingly early contractions by singing along – admirably loudly – to every track that Magic FM was playing on the radio only inches from the laminated sign stating that music was not to be played aloud on the ward.

It was the morning of the 2017 London Marathon, and as I waited for my white-carb breakfast and the 'midwife with the longest fingers' to try and 'get things going', I was idly following along on Twitter as the runners assembled in Greenwich at the starting line. I was determined not to tweet, for fear of my long-awaited animal self saying something in the wild abandon of childbirth that I would later regret, but I could watch. Oh, I could watch.

I searched for runners who had contacted me over the preceding months, and silently wished them luck, checking their posted selfies to see that their hair was tied back properly, their tops not so loose that they'd chafe later. I checked on contemporaries who were running a second or third marathon, and envied how vigorous, how primed they must feel. I checked on celebrities, trying to work out who'd struggled, who looked strong, who were this year's stars. And I looked at the official shots from the marathon: that familiar snake of neon and adrenaline, taken from above as thousands lined up ready to run, a seething mass of hope, grief and potential.

I had drawn imagined parallels between marathons and childbirth for years. As I had turned that final corner on the Mall with my friend Julia six years before, her triumphant cry had rung out that, 'This feels like the bit when the baby finally comes out!' I had discussed it endlessly with my sister, who had reassured me that, 'Just at the very moment you are convinced you cannot go on a second longer, that, THAT is the time when you are a moment away from the best bit.' And I had tried to navigate birth plans and medical appointments with marathon-running in mind – it was the only comparison I had. I knew I could take pain and put in hard work for longer than I had ever imagined was possible. As I saw the familiar dinosaur costumes and heard Ron Goodwin's 'The Trap', the London Marathon theme music, I hugged to my chest the knowledge that I could outlast my own expectations. I possessed a secret weapon: endurance.

Yet there was jealousy as I saw those bodies flying past with every flick of my thumb. Yes, I longed to glow as they did, so fit and healthy, so lithe and limber. I felt something like fury at the fluidity of their movement, the excitement and apprehension in their tweets. I wanted to be able to stand on one leg and stretch, feeling blood pushed up and along the fronts of my thighs and the backs of my calves. I yearned to just jog on the spot for no other reason than to stay a little warmer. Oh, I hated them all. I wanted to live in a body I recognised as my own again. Was this bubbling fury my animal self emerging?

No.

Another day passed. We enjoyed another visit from the long-fingered midwife, who remained confident she could somehow break my waters. I say 'somehow', but by now I knew how, as I felt her scrape around the edges of my aching cervix while I concentrated on the view.

We were advised to take a walk around the hospital: *Perhaps some stairs would help? But don't leave the grounds!* I had no intention of staying in the hospital. We walked to the seafront and sat on a bench I had used to stretch my hamstrings on countless long runs. The same bench I would sit on, typing into my phone, in six months' time. I thought of the marathon runners, now surely crossing the finish line long before I would. We walked back up the steep hill to the hospital. Still nothing. My head felt as if it might pop off with the exertion. Pressure continued to rise within me.

The next morning the obstetrician told me that they would like to consider a Caesarean section. I had barely slept for two days, my blood pressure was starting to put both my baby and my heart under unnecessary strain, and I longed for my own bed. But I was anxious about further medical intervention, particularly if it wasn't strictly necessary. I was also concerned about somehow being lazy: if I consented to a Caesarean, was I taking the easy option, becoming a bystander in my own birth story? When would I be a part of this process, rather than a human box file carrying the decisions of multiple doctors? The obstetrician stressed that I didn't *have* to have the surgery, but that if I chose not to, I would need to stay in hospital to keep my heart monitored. So when it was put to me that the best thing I could do for my health was to go home for the night, sleep well, and come back for the operation tomorrow morning, I surrendered.

The next day, the one on which my baby was born, the sky was a limitless blue. The operating theatre in which I had my Caesarean section was on the fifteenth floor of the hospital, with a view of the sea and beyond, all the way to the horizon. I lay flat on the bed, immobilised from the ribcage down. I had never had more than a minor local anaesthetic before, and watched with fascination as the surgical team lifted my legs from bed to operating table as if they were coiled bundles of rope being heaved across a ship's deck. Prince's 'Raspberry Beret' was playing on a radio in a corner of the room. A sailing boat slowly bisected the window as the knife cut open the first of my seven layers. For one of the most important moments of my life, one which has had an impact on every day since, I felt almost nothing. A rummage, a tug, some polite chat to distract me.

The surgeon yanked at what I assumed was . . . me? It was as if he were trying to unravel wet bedlinen, tangled from the spin of the washing machine.

'Alexandra, do you know what a bicornate uterus is? Some call it a heart-shaped womb.'

'No,' I replied. 'Why?'

It turns out that my womb is the shape of a heart. It has a deep indentation at the top, cleaving it almost in two. You wouldn't notice unless you were looking for the distortion. It only revealed itself once I was there, on the operating table. The implied romance of the malformation's name is far outweighed by the potential danger it can present to both parent and baby. But since that morning, I think of it often, my heart-shaped uterus. It strikes me as typical of our relationships with our bodies: a problem discreetly hidden, only discovered once urgent, and perhaps harmful.

A tug as the surgeon explained this to me. A yank as he looked up.

'This little one has been growing in one side only, and now they are pretty firmly wedged in.' My baby. All those nights I'd clutched my belly, convinced the baby wasn't moving. They simply couldn't, for lack of space.

The rummaging continued for some time. I tried to concentrate on my breathing, as 'Raspberry Beret' slid into The Bangles' 'Manic Monday'. Isn't it Tuesday? I wondered.

'Well, I have some good news for you,' said the surgeon. 'You can put aside any anxieties you might have had about indulging in an unnecessary procedure. Your umbilical cord has several knots in it. This and the way this little one is so firmly wedged in means that you would always have ended up here. At least you've done it on a good night's sleep.'

My eyes slid up to the ceiling. Another tug. Good news had meant so many different things this last year, I barely knew how to register this latest piece of information.

A sudden flurry seemed to gather at my feet. Muttering, shuffling, the addition of a couple more staff. A pause. D and I stared at each other, holding hands around the cannula coming out of the back of my hand. We didn't dare speak. Our eyes locked, both of us wondering what was going on. I could see the shoulders of one of the team move. One of their arms seemed to be rubbing vigorously. Suddenly, a yelp. The tiny newborn cry that D and I had been referring to as 'the seagulls' each time we had heard a newborn on the ward that week. Now at last, our seagull was here.

'You have a beautiful son, Alexandra, we're just giving him a bit of help to get breathing before we cut that cord.'

A son. And not yet mine. For five agonising minutes the nurses had him on their side of the room while I lay there – naked, numbed, immobile – waiting to begin the mothering.

When the baby was finally put in my arms I wasn't afraid, I wasn't relieved, I wasn't overwhelmed. I felt as if it were me who had come home, not him.

It was you all along, I thought as I stared at his swollen scowl, D hugging both of us. A perfect, furious peach, and one I had surely known for my entire life. All of those other attempts, each needle, each procedure, each embryo – now it seemed perfectly obvious that they would never have worked. Because it was him who was our baby, and we had just had to wait. I thought of how much he and I had been through already, wanting to apologise for Professor Nicolaides's vicious needle, for all that pressure I had put on his heart on the train, for all those nights I had been awake worrying. But I didn't. Because in an instant I felt entirely different. Where I had felt terror that he'd leave, now I had absolute faith in him.

This sense of total trust in the baby never really left me. We struggled to breastfeed, but I found pumping milk incredibly easy. I had always looked forward to breastfeeding, having spent at least the last two decades feeling encumbered by my out-of-proportion boobs. I had devoted pages to them, and how to manage running with them, and even when the IVF with its months of progesterone suppositories had made them even bigger I still had faith that one day, somehow, they would prove useful. How could I not be a natural breastfeeder? I had blithely whispered to myself through every class, every midwife discussion, every chat with my sister. But I wasn't. My hungry little baby could get no purchase on my flat dinner-plate nipples, and was appalled by the nipple shields I tried to use. But he seized the bottles full of milk I produced, his urgent mouth latching on to them as if he were made to do it.

But just as that sense of utter trust in the baby, that sense of having known him all along was developing, the very opposite seemed to be happening between me and D. We had been through so much together by this point, and during it all D had been an exceptionally loving husband. More than that, D had not merely been a good person, but the one *I* needed *for me.* D paid attention, an excellent judge of when to listen to my worries and when to gently point out that I was exhausted, that it would all feel better in the morning. D had known when to take me seriously; when discussing things properly would help; and when simply being silly with me, teasing me and goofing around over bedtime teeth-brushing was all the distraction I would need. I had never felt less than completely supported, but also I had felt *noticed.* But since we had returned from the hospital, I felt something close to invisible.

It was not that I was being ignored, because on so many levels, my every need was being met. But there was something about D's behaviour, which while always tender, was somehow never quite meeting my gaze. An essential connection was fraying, and each time D offered to take over with the minutiae of looking after L, as we had named the baby, I felt a few more threads stretch and snap. Where was my soulmate going, right before my very eyes?

'Don't worry about it,' D would tell me, as I sat behind the breast pump, longing to hold my baby. 'He's getting the milk anyway, so you just relax.'

And D was right. Oh, how many mothers long to be told to take it easy! But I *wanted* to breastfeed. I wanted the closeness, the convenience, and above all I wanted to feel that my body was doing what it was born to do. I felt short-changed by my experience, my time behind the pump, but somehow unable to argue under the weight of D's ceaseless offers of help. Everything looked the same, but everything felt different.

Because D's help wasn't all that I wanted. I was also yearning for a grain of that previous attentiveness. Sure, I was being given a lot of help now, but I was left grasping at air when I tried to snatch a little of the affection, approval or even the acknowledgement that had once been lavished on me.

We had done it, made this epic achievement. And despite all the hurdles thrown in our path. We had stayed together where so many other couples were broken apart by IVF, and I wanted to celebrate that, to celebrate *us*. My inbox was a constant flow of congratulations from friends, family and even readers as they heard my happy news after what they now knew had been such a grim and lonely journey for the two of us. But the one I wanted to hear it from the most now seemed the furthest away.

I longed to be held tight and told I was superwoman. I wanted to be told that my body was a miracle, that it was more desirable than ever now that we had witnessed what it could really do. I yearned to be seen, but D now seemed only to have eyes for parenthood. Sure, I wanted the bottles to be sterilised and neatly stored before we settled down for the evening. But I would have happily done it myself twice as many times if only I could be pressed against the countertop of our tiny galley kitchen, irresistible, and told that I was a wonder. It would have been worth a thousand neatly stacked teats, each one further evidence of what I couldn't do. Why was kindness starting to feel so cruel?

Let Dad help, they would say at the classes, in the books, on the blogs. *It helps him to feel involved, and you can rest!*

It was perfectly valid advice. And I did want to rest. Even turning my body in bed entailed a few minutes of radiating pain, throbbing brutally like a force field around me. But I felt possessive over the baby – I wanted him to *want* to latch on to me. I didn't want him to be fine with a plastic bottle and a different parent. After all I had been through, how was I not . . . essential? Time and again I would feel the baby taken out of my arms, a bottle presented to him. I would wake up with a start, my breasts aching and swollen, my T-shirt already dripping with milk. I would woozily hurry to the breast pump only to discover the baby happily guzzling on a bottle – a bottle full of *my* milk, I would think to myself – in the arms of his other parent.

But how to object to this? It was a freedom breastfeeding mothers dream of, a connection single mothers longed for their children to have with their other parent! A respite from night feeds, my aching scar, my fuzzy brain; my distended breasts were urgently encouraging. But my heart. I wanted to hold my baby to my breast. I wanted to hear it in his cry: *I want you, I long for you, you and no other will do.*

It never came. And so I smiled. I smiled and thanked D, and tried to shuffle past this selfish longing to be part of their happy set-up. To be jealous of someone helping me was daft, I told myself as I flicked the switch on the pump, heard the bovine whirring of the suction begin and watched what looked increasingly less like a helpful husband and more like a glowing Madonna and child at the other end of the sofa. Was D helping me or aping me? I started to wonder.

And so it was that within weeks of the baby's birth, the very oxygen I breathed seemed to be of a different quality. I am not talking about the magic of parenthood. I am talking about how my sense of self, and then my actual reality, started to shift and slide beneath my feet.

It was imperceptible at first. Like when you're sitting on a stationary train, parallel to another. You see the faces next door slowly start to move away from you and for a heartbeat you're not sure if your train has departed the station or theirs. A flicker of doubt, a moment's disorientation, before the truth hoves clearly into view.

For a while, I thought maybe it was just tiredness. The health visitors told me to expect it, especially after a relatively complicated birth. The first time one came, I refused to look at my C-section scar, or even consider removing the dressing. I was terrified of that scar, not understanding how the pain could be so superficial and yet so deep. It was tiny, and so low, well below even the line of the most daring pair of bikini bottoms. But sitting up in bed, turning to lift a mug from a side table, reaching for a high cupboard – how did these things create tugs of hot pain which felt so far beneath the surface? When I asked the midwife if that sounded normal she breezily told me that yes, it was quite normal.

'Don't forget they cut through seven layers,' she said. 'Well, I say cut . . . but these days they rip the muscle, as studies have shown that when it's ragged it heals faster, meshes together better.'

I blanched. 'Rip?'

'Yes,' a cheery smile. 'Like pulled pork!'

As she left, she warned me that I wouldn't have the option to not look at it next time she visited. 'That scar is part of your body now, and you have to learn to accept it if not love it,' she told me, her gaze steady while I tried to look anywhere but her eyes.

Forty-eight hours later she lay me on my bed, before gently removing the dressing, helping me up, and guiding me to the full-length mirror on my bedroom wall.

'There you go,' she said softly. 'It's not too bad, is it?'

And it wasn't. It was less than half the size I had imagined it would be, albeit livid, with spider-leg stitches still sticking out in places.

'Touch it,' she told me. 'Gently though.'

I looked at her, uncertain. I was afraid I would rip open again.

'Go on . . .' And so I did, running my finger along the raised edge of the scar, surprised to realise how numb the area still was. I had expected pain but I just felt a blurry nothingness. I had thought a touch might cause the stitches to burst open, gore spurting everywhere, but I remained intact. Sealed up nicely. At least there. At least physically.

We had a steady but not unmanageable flow of visitors, from friends to family, each of them bringing their own news, their individual responses to the baby, and the simple distraction of their presence. When they had left, we carried on working our way through the box sets we had been saving for early parenthood, taking life slowly as we got to know the baby, and recovered from the drama of the last few weeks and months. At last, we were living the nesting dream, the treasured moments which only a year ago had been a fantasy. It was May, and Brighton was at its best. The trees in bloom, the beach not yet heaving, the festival giving the city a sort of buzzy optimism that had seemed unthinkable six months earlier as winter had closed in on us during that long wait for the test results.

We went on walks across parks as they exploded with greenery, flowers and posters for fringe events due to begin hours after our new bedtime. We worked out which coffee shops had space for the buggy while we shared pastries and waited patiently while fellow diners admired the baby. We took endless photos of his tiny feet at rest, his frown in slumber, his surprise at the discovery of bathtime. And we sent them to each other from just the other side of the room, before spending ten minutes discussing how wonderful every eyelash, every toenail, every fold of fat was.

But in the quiet moments when the baby was asleep and the television was off, there was a lack of connection between us that I was unable to diagnose. Without the baby to either cosset or discuss, the air between us became thin, leaving me sipping for oxygen. I felt a strange competitiveness that seemed both pointless and consuming. I didn't dare to articulate it to anyone, but I wondered if D too was feeling a sense of jealousy. All that focus on me through the IVF, the pregnancy, book promotion and then the birth itself. That is a long time to spend in a chair, slightly stage left, as the star of the show has lights literally focused on her innermost self. Had D grown as tired of watching me bear that burden as I had grown of bearing it? Was this a grab for centre stage? Because if it was, D's ease with the baby while I was still struggling physically left me envious of their time together, a leading lady wondering if her time had passed, just as she had expected to enjoy the spotlight a little longer.

Something is curdling in our happy home, I began to realise as I hid the bottles of breast milk at the back of the fridge where I hoped D would not spot them. I wanted to be the one to give L *my* milk, I thought as my petulant finger flicked bottles of sterilised water – neatly prepared by D earlier in the evening – to the front. *Let* me *be the mother.*

Then, just as fast, *This mendacity is needless. Who am I becoming, when I have everything I wanted?*

Morning after morning I would wake, better rested than any other mother I knew, to find L and D happy without me. I could not enjoy it. Just as everyone – from family to my readers – believed me to be as happy as I could possibly be, a deep sense of disquiet was thrumming through my still-ragged body. I had a kind, willing and super-hands-on husband but all I could see was a cuckoo in my nest.

I had long thought that the happiness I would feel once I became a mother would be pure. Like an expensive vodka, its bottle perfectly smooth, glistening with condensation. Potent, but with clarity. But this feeling was sticky. Still powerful, still love – of course! SO much love. But this happiness was dark, thick with tannins, swirling with a murky hit at the back of my throat and a constant promise of tomorrow's sickly hangover.

Perhaps it was my profound sense of unease with my own body that was behind this. I wanted to be proud of it and all it had done. I wanted to be that same woman who had stood up in front of crowds of hundreds, inspiring them about how we must love what our bodies can do for us, and not what they can do for others. I longed to be the gleaming Instagram mum jiggling her belly next to a sponsored product, waxing lyrical about the strength she never knew she had until parenthood. I yearned to feel as if I actually lived inside this body I saw as I looked down in the bath.

Instead, it seemed that my body and I had not been invited to the same party, let alone everyone else. I had been pulled apart like pork yet there was still no sign of my stomach muscles doing anything close to healing once you looked even a couple of millimetres below the surface. When I crossed the road with the pram and tried to engage my core in order to push the front wheels up and onto the kerb I felt nothing. Where I could once tense and shove a buggy forward, now my core was doing nothing beyond making a mouthless, blank-eyed emoji face at me. But still I shuffled on.

Or perhaps this relentless creep of unease was entirely external. After all, the first few months of L's life saw a torrent of bad news, often breaking during the night. The Manchester bomb, the London Bridge attacks, the Grenfell fire. Every bedtime, every late-night pumping session, every 2 a.m. bottle left me clammy with dread about what might happen if I turned on the TV or looked at my phone. Outside our four walls, the world seemed to be exploding in hate, the vulnerable flailing unaided. I sobbed for days about the newborns made homeless in Notting

Hill, bagging up as many baby clothes as I could and sending them to the church halls listed on the news. I sobbed for hours watching Ariana Grande's One Love Manchester concert, fretful about how I could ever keep L safe in a world which seemed to be turning itself inside out. Every time news broke I felt more aware of how lucky I was. And yet more miserable.

Perhaps it was the intermittent calls from the police about the assault on the train that were setting me on edge. At first I was told that the defendant would be representing himself in court, and therefore able to cross-examine me directly. Then that someone else would be hired to ask questions composed by the defendant. Then there was a call about dates, and one about timings, and one about whether or not I would like to visit the court beforehand. Could I bring my baby? I asked. Yes, I could. But did I want to? I was left thinking. Had he not absorbed enough cortisol in every mouthful of the milk I was so doggedly still pumping for him every day?

Or perhaps it was simply that my two greatest coping mechanisms – running and swimming – had been whisked away from me. I waited eagerly for my fabled 'six-week check', looking forward to having my GP assess whether I was ready for either. Desperate for the all-clear, I was left a little limp-hearted when the appointment focused on the baby. His hips were examined at length and there was no shortage of cuddles and congratulations – it was after all the same GP who had referred us for IVF nearly three years previously, and she was visibly thrilled that despite the waiting lists, setbacks and heartaches we had encountered en route, we had hit the jackpot. But the check on me was brief.

'. . . and how are you? Any tears?' was the bulk of it.

'Do you find yourself still able to laugh?' she added after enquiring if my scar was healing nicely. I thought of the photograph D had taken of L photoshopped as if talking to Charlie Brown and nodded enthusiastically. 'Oh yes!' I replied, as if a sticker might be in it for me like at those dentist visits in childhood.

I showed her my scar, received congratulations that my blood pressure was finally back to normal, and we tickled the baby again. My pelvic floor went unmentioned. The results of carrying a growing baby for nine months in an entirely lopsided womb went unmentioned. I was given the OK to swim.

The next day D took care of L while I headed straight into the sea. The summer was turning out to be one long heatwave, and it was a full-time job trying to keep the baby cool. My body also felt constantly overheated and sticky – from holding the baby, holding the plastic of the pump to me, holding it all together. I longed for the cool salt water as I hobbled my way down Brighton's shelf of pebbles towards the sea. I submerged myself as soon as the water was deep enough, but when I came back up to the surface I was consumed by panic, reeling at the expansive view after spending so long in small dark rooms – pumping, feeding, lulling. The bigger problem was that my core muscles were still so weak that I had absolutely no manoeuvrability. I couldn't tip myself back to see further afield, I couldn't turn myself to swim home towards shore, I couldn't do anything but bob up and down, entirely at the mercy of the water. At first I was terrified, immediately returned to the gasping horror of my first swimming lesson, three years earlier. Absolutely out of control, I was unmoored from the me I thought I would comfortably be returning to by now. I was dependent on the strength of my arms to do a sort of standing breaststroke, and the goodwill of the sea to at some point return me to land. After a minute or two I relaxed into it, surrendered to the bobbing. Eventually my arms and the tide returned me to the pebbles where I scrabbled ashore to my waiting possessions. I had made it back into the sea that day, but I was far from being back to swimming. I hadn't even been able to get myself into a horizontal swimming position, and I couldn't see that happening any time soon. It was another dent in my sense of ownership over my own body. Each was invisible, but together they meant that pressure was mounting up, wearing me thinner and thinner.

I also needed to run, but after carrying the baby in such a lopsided position, my pelvis was in no fit state for the high impact of running. After the six-week check I spent a small fortune on going to see a postnatal physiotherapist, where I was strongly advised that I should not run until at least November. To be told this in June left me crumpled and unfocused. My weight gain was huge. It was exhausting to carry myself around. My thighs rubbed in the heat and I looked babyish in maternity wear but could not do up any waisted trousers.

I tried to walk, feeling my pelvis slip and crunch, unbalanced unless I was clinging to the front bar of the pram as if it were a Zimmer frame. It was a slow but thorough untethering of me from my physical self. The building blocks I had used to create a body and mind that worked together as a coherent self I could recognise and be proud of, were turning to rubble around me. I wasn't just carrying the extra weight of a baby, my back twingeing each time I picked him up as my core struggled to support me, I was also carrying the weight of a self I didn't recognise at all.

I was shuffling through life in what felt like a suit of armour that no longer seemed fit for purpose. The day the physio told me I had a long wait until I could run again I went home and cried. I cried a lot, between the visitors who poured into the house proclaiming how wonderful it must be to finally have everything I had ever wanted. I even cried on the physio herself, mourning the body which I had once fought so hard for, and which had gifted me so much joy.

'You've simply become unbalanced,' she told me, her index finger tapping my chest, her other thumb in the small of my back. 'You need to learn how to walk straight again.' As I wiped my eyes, sitting on the edge of her physio bench, I knew it was beyond me to even try and explain how inadvertently insightful she was being.

And yet, in between all this, there were moments of happiness that only a couple of years ago I had thought would be forever out of my reach. The older and more alert L became, the more fun he was to have around, and when it was just the two of us I was often more confident that we were not merely coping but that I was loved. Every time we left the house for one of our 'adventures' my heart skipped with the glee I felt at the prospect of spending time with him. To the supermarket for me to show him brightly coloured fruit and veg while he squealed with delight, to visit a friend who would carry him around their garden, showing him flowers and letting him pet the dog, to swimming lessons where half an hour of dips and swooshes left us both exhausted by the excitement of it all, yet humming with the oxytocin high of our skin-to-skin contact.

The three of us had fun as well. D was endlessly inventive with games, funny voices at storytime, dens made of sofa cushions and swings made of picnic blankets. Babies are so absurd, it was impossible to spend time with the two of them and not be cheered by the silliness of a baby propped up as if reading the Sunday papers. I made new friends with other women who had had babies at similar times. And old friends revelled in the funny photos I would send, the chance to finally dispense wisdom on teething, sleep training and where to buy the best elasticated trousers for a maternity leave well spent. How long I had laboured under the illusion that happiness could fill a space, entirely untouched by anxiety, grief or confusion. How easy it was proving to live with all three, shifting and sliding like the moving walkways found between airport gates, propelling me from one to the other.

Then, a fresh blip. In what seemed like a final bodily act of betrayal, when L hit four months I was hit by a vicious bout of the shingles virus. Weakened by the IVF, the pregnancy and the silent battle I seemed to be fighting with both body and heart, my immune system rolled over and let the virus in, a fizzing sharpness attacking one side of my neck and head.

When I first went to the GP I was told that the excruciating pain was simply muscle strain in my neck, very common in new mothers who tend to carry and nurse on one side more than the other. A few days later, when the blisters started to loop around one side of my head, deep in my hair and blowing one ear up like a rugby player's, I was reluctantly given a diagnosis of shingles. Again, it felt as if what was happening to my body was being disputed by the experts around me. I knew what muscle pain felt like, I had spent enough time training and lifting weights to know what a muscle strain was. And I knew what position I held L in, how I lulled him to sleep.

Why was I consistently being deemed the least reliable witness of my own reality? Being told I was not carrying my own baby, being told there was no hand on my behind, being told those sharp electric prickles were muscle strain. I swung between fury at being belittled this way and murmurs of self-doubt that perhaps I was wrong: I was an unreliable narrator of my own situation, I could not be trusted.

The only cure for the shingles was rest. More bloody rest! But the more I rest the less I see of the baby, I wanted to explain. And I'm already beginning to suspect that I am doing a terrible job in comparison to my husband! And lo, the less I saw of the baby the more of a failure I felt. My precious milk began to dry up, the urgent suck of the pump straining as it retrieved less and less until I finally gave up for a week. Even the slightest draught on my neck sent a tidal wave of electric pinpricks across my skin. Brushing my hair was unbearable, so I left it, wetting it from time to time to try and stem the buzzing blisters, each one a fresh electric zap on a skull that seemed to be slowly peeling away from my brain.

I was exhausted. And I still hadn't worked out what was wrong. I knew that this was not postnatal depression, because I knew the difference between depression and sadness. But the fog of sadness was getting thicker and thicker, meaning that pinpointing its cause became harder and harder. And still the tectonic plates of reality seemed to be shifting and sliding around me.

4

One morning I stood at the door to the sitting room, freshly awake, my hair sticking up, semi-crusted with shingles blisters.

'How long have you guys been up?' I asked, as I bent down to kiss L, who was sitting, playing with his toes on D's lap.

'An hour or two,' came the calm reply.

'Oh God, I'm so sorry, you must have to get to work,' I said.

'Don't worry, you've been really ill,' D reassured me. I wasn't worried about what time D went to work, I was worried about L having more fun with his cheery, good-in-the-mornings parent than with his bedraggled, falling-apart-at-the-seams parent.

We had a little chat about feed times, plans for the day, whether I would cope and when D might be able to get home that evening. I tried to calm my beating heart, to orientate myself in the day, to scrabble around in my memory for the plans I had made for us, for the fun we might be able to have. I babbled, explaining what we would be up to, as D leaned in to kiss me goodbye.

'Is that foundation you're wearing?' I asked, as D turned to leave the room.

'Sunblock!' came the reply, over a shoulder, followed by the slam of the front door.

Fair enough, I thought. It was a heatwave summer and D had very fair skin. Anyway, what if it was foundation? It was hardly unheard of. Perhaps this scrutiny was just another manifestation of my growing jealousy about who was coping best with the baby.

And yet. A small voice whispered. A couple of years ago, D wearing foundation might have meant a fun trip to the MAC store, the two of us feeling conspiratorial as we tested samples together. Me feeling indulgent, not a little endeared by the idea of a husband who was so happy to flout conventionality. Now, as I wiped the orangey brown smear of . . . sunblock? from L's cheek, it all seemed to feel a lot less like a shared confidence, and a lot more like a secret.

A couple of weeks later we went to London for the day. It hadn't been the easiest night, sleep-wise, but we were all looking forward to it. Buggy parks had been researched, museum opening times double-checked and Southern Rail timetables scrutinised in order to avoid football crowds. On that third point, we were outsmarted when a stag do boarded the train at Gatwick.

I was still very nervous on crowded trains, particularly if groups of men were in the carriage, dominating the mood. It would still be some time before my heart didn't start to hammer at the memory of being trapped, pregnant, in that first-class carriage, those pairs of knees turned to block my path out. D sensed my discomfort and tried to make space for me, reaching to move bags and jackets to the shelf above us. In the kerfuffle, keys, coins and a colourful plastic tube came tumbling out of pockets, past our heads and onto the floor. D was flustered, scrabbling around to retrieve belongings while the stags talked around us, sipping from their cans, the scent of their going-out aftershaves overwhelming us.

I watched as the coloured tube rolled under a wheel of the pram. I managed to bend down to pick it up, and as I stood I turned it over in my hand. It was a tube of BB cream. Not the fanciest, but nor was it one you would buy without doing a bit of research. Sure, it contained SPF, but essentially it was make-up. Is this what D had been wearing the other week? I looked up. It was what D was wearing now.

Why lie? Why lie to me, D? But I said nothing. I swallowed it down. I was used to it now, this feeling of being reassured that something wasn't happening when I was increasingly convinced that it was. The common denominator seemed to be me, so perhaps – I found myself thinking yet again – *I* was the one who was wrong after all.

Why was I so upset by seeing a tube of BB cream? This was who I had chosen, and willingly, adoringly married: an unconventional man. Someone who would not impose stereotypes on me any more than they would on themselves or their son. This refusal to see gender in an ordinary way was absolutely one of the most attractive things about D. We had long agreed that gender was a stifling straitjacket for all but the few who sit happily at the extremes of their respective points on the spectrum. While I rarely shaved my legs, D often had painted nails. While I mostly wear chinos or jeans with sweatshirts, D often liked to wear interesting asymmetric clothing and even things from women's clothing brands. While I longed for a life of adventure akin to my hero George Plimpton, D revered

Alexander McQueen. None of this was new; in fact, it had very much been the point, especially when we had come to thinking about becoming parents. I wanted a parent who would let L know that the parameters of what he could be were wide open, just as they were for me.

Before the pregnancy, D had stood shoulder to shoulder with me, in firm agreement that women were no less women if they did not have children, whether it was through choice or circumstance. We were not to be defined by mere biology, we were who we said we were, we were our experiences, our hopes and our pain, and we had to be respected for that. This absolute clarity, this unselfconscious agreement, this sense of being twin souls on the matter was at the very heart of our love, what had made me feel so treasured during what I had thought were my darkest hours. It wasn't a quirk: it was the foundation stone on which our marriage was built.

When our luck changed and we prepared for parenthood, we had agreed that we would be doing any child of ours a huge disservice if we brought them up within the claustrophobic parameters that society prescribed for children – whether it be a baby boy dressed only in blue or a girl with an absurd bow on her bald head to indicate some sort of gaudy femininity. We had deliberately elected not to know the sex of the baby when I was pregnant – as much to stem a potential tide of opinion from family and professionals as to keep a surprise for ourselves. (Midwives still took it upon themselves to tell me I was carrying 'a footballer' every time a movement was felt, asking if I would be happy with a boy – as if a footballer couldn't be a girl, or girls somehow did not move prenatally.)

Why was I now wanting to slam these doors of possibility shut, scrabbling for certainties when I had previously yearned for the widest possible spectrum of acceptable behaviours from all of us? What was wrong with me that I suddenly wanted things so neat, so narrow, so easy? Particularly as so much of D's behaviour had seemed to be to do with a passion for colour and design as much as self-expression or gender itself.

After all, I had barely batted an eyelid when, the previous summer, D had returned home with hair both undercut and dyed white-blonde. I remember thinking that it seemed flamboyant for someone who was otherwise happy to sit back, who was rarely the centre of attention, but it had seemed like a little more than that. A cry for attention? An ineffective one, particularly as I thought it looked pretty good. A reach for femininity? No, really, it was as androgynous, as 'Brighton', as so much else about D's look, which had always been specific, considered, stylish – while I had spent much of the day in sports kit.

It was no secret that D had made my life more beautiful the minute we became a couple, helping me to fit blinds, amend hem lengths and choose lipsticks. When we first met, my home was defined by heaps of books, washing I was convinced I would fold and put away before needing to wear it again, and plants that deserved 'just a couple more weeks' before I officially declared them dead.

I was fascinated by a mind that saw the world in shapes and colours rather than words and ideas. D would look at a photography book to relax in the same way that I would read a pacy thriller. D would rearrange the sitting room, able to visualise how it would look beforehand, whereas I needed to spend a sweaty Saturday morning pushing sofas from side to side until I could even begin to imagine what furniture would fit which space. D could hang pictures with apparent ease – and had been quick to replace so much of what was on my walls ('Why do you only have words and sayings up here? All you do is read all day anyway?') with colourful prints, dramatic seascapes and interesting photographs. How the world looked had transformed for me when D had stepped into it – and with that my own appearance had changed as I glowed, relaxing into the love I felt so palpably. So why was I now begrudging the degree to which D's own look was polished? Particularly when, following the mayhem my own body had been through, I was so preoccupied by my own outward appearance?

Since L had arrived, I was increasingly sure that D's unconventionality had begun to seem more furtive, where once it had been celebratory. A few months earlier I had got into bed and noticed that D had shaved legs. They felt undeniably lovely. To snuggle in alongside legs which felt as satisfyingly smooth as my own did when I (rarely) bothered to shave them was a pleasant surprise, a tactile pleasure. But as I had giggled and asked why, D flinched.

'It just feels better like that,' came the answer. 'Why do you even care?'

'I don't!' I had quickly joked. 'I just wish you'd offered to do mine too.'

But I had peeled away. Then checked myself. It wasn't my body. If D were to afford me the space to have legs in whatever state of smoothness I chose, it was surely only fair if I did the same. Yet that flinch stayed with me. The defensiveness, as if D had expected me to recoil.

What did it matter? I had told myself. It was millimetres of hair. Cyclists would have got rid of it. Footballers might have got rid of it. Half the male cast of *Love Island* would probably have got rid of it. Many people, including men, practise so many varieties of waxing, shaving and plucking these days that it is almost impossible to read anything into it, and even the most sophisticated readings would probably reveal more about class, current male role models or passing influencer fashions than actual gender. So what had made me so uneasy?

Now, faced with the BB cream, I tried to examine my response to this behaviour, truly asking what I was uncomfortable with, and why. Perhaps, I told myself, it would reveal truths about my sense of self that I would rather not confront when feeling so dissociated and unattractive so soon after childbirth.

It felt as if my thoughts on the matter were caught in an eternal Möbius strip: I would fret about the importance D was placing on physical attributes, talk myself into remembering that this was who D had always been, before starting to pick at my own misery about my body, then reprimanding myself for such thoughts, looking at what was causing it, and taking the easy loop back to examining D's behaviour. Each time I thought I had consoled myself, my mind would turn another corner of the loop, ending up where I had started.

Was what I had been seeing as D struggling for L's attention, in fact a struggle to be seen a certain way? A more feminine way? Was D's competitiveness nothing to do with my having been the focus for so long, but because I was being seen as female-bodied? Was the very thing which had left me feeling so constrained and exhausted – my body – the same thing that had been prompting this behaviour in D?

Alongside the sadness and the exhaustion that were now starting to wallop me from all sides was a tangy sort of guilt. How on earth did I have time – with all that had and still was going on – to fret about the curve of my husband's eyebrows, the softness of my husband's legs, the precise consistency of my husband's suncream or BB cream or foundation? What was wrong with me that these things were causing any concern, when we had spent so long discussing – and agreeing! – that the definition of what a man could be needed to be broadened just as much as that of what made a woman?

I did have time for this fretting though. I found that time at 3 a.m. as I lay in the dark listening to the baby breathe in his cot, at 10 a.m. while I waited for the kettle to boil, staring out of the kitchen window wondering when I might feel something close to hope again, and at 6 p.m. when D came home from work and ran straight to the baby, unable to make any eye contact with me at all. What had I done to deserve this, to feel so *avoided*? I can see now that what lay behind all that evasion was quite simply shame: months', years', decades' worth of shame rushing up and out of someone who had done so well compressing it for so long. But what I saw then was a husband who had somewhere else to look. A husband who was choosing not to see me at all.

One afternoon I found myself sobbing as I hung out endless muslin cloths on the washing line, remembering a moment a few days after L was born: I had been lying on the sofa, looking at my phone, the Moses basket on the floor next to me. D had walked past the door to the sitting room and muttered quietly, 'Oh my GOD, I love you so much it hurts.'

'Thank you!' I had replied.

'Oh, I was talking to the baby,' came the reply. Shame drenched those words as they left D's lips, not intended cruelly. But the effect was no less cruel.

And still I felt guilty. I had done my research, I knew that bringing a baby into a relationship could cause turmoil with the emotions of its parents. I knew how isolating it could potentially be for a father, how difficult it could be to bond with a baby whose daily routine was so dependent on its mother. And I knew how frustrating the IVF process had been for D as I had been the focus time and again, while D was left passive, that one solitary moment of genuine usefulness so very fleeting.

D was still kind and loving and attentive to the family and the house. We still enjoyed our time together, laughed and adored the baby together, made plans for our future together. We were, in almost all areas, fantastic communicators. We could thrash out financial plans and worries without bringing guilt or recriminations into it. We could discuss a film or an exhibition's merits for a whole train trip back from London, happily disagreeing on angles without taking it personally. We went through the process of investigating, visiting and then selecting nurseries for L without falling out – our views aligned in what we were looking for. We were a team, and D's goodness was obvious to me daily. Meanwhile, we were awash with love for L, who continued to be an easy baby with an apparently never-ending supply of smiles. He fell into a sleeping routine with relative ease, he snuggled into the arms of adoring friends and relatives without a whimper, and he seemed delighted by every minute of it.

So I told myself that this would pass. Of *course* I was being hypersensitive to things – I had been through so much, and was so exhausted by it all. I would repeat this to myself again and again, that Möbius strip of anxious thoughts curling up again, nice and tight if I simply tried hard enough. But then, just as often, I would try to catch D's eye for a moment, only to feel that gaze, that true eye-to-eye contact, slip away yet again – and the strip would snap open, the path leading only one way.

I searched for new ways to connect with D, increasingly desperate to feel the sort of honest, intuitive bond we had shared so effortlessly only months before, and threw myself into cooking. Cooking had been my saviour a decade before, after a grim triple whammy of adult mumps, a traffic accident and a bad break-up. Newly freelance, I spent a summer going loopy at home, sliding into a melancholy which skirted and then became mild depression, before going to work part-time at Divertimenti Cookery School. I was an enthusiastic but possibly less than effective employee. It was an age before social media (I can remember discovering YouTube for the first time at my little desk at the back of the Marylebone High Street store) and to be a foodie was significantly more of a commitment than flinging a snap of a matcha latte online. I took bookings for the classes and was charged with ordering the ingredients for each one.

Finding rose water or pomegranate molasses meant a trip up Edgware Road on my Vespa, finding a certain type of matzo meant a scoot to Panzer's in Swiss Cottage, and to get fresh yeast for the baking class I would have to walk into Patisserie Valerie and ask nicely if we could have a little of theirs. Being up, dressed and out of the house for five hours of sensory stimulation – checking which peaches were ripe, making sure the correct herbs had arrived, unpacking the fish from James Knight of Mayfair – had helped to get my head straight at a time when I was nursing an injury and was still a couple of years away from discovering the comforts of a long solitary run on a blustery day, or an icy swim after a sleepless night. The gentle alchemy of creating a mood from flavours and textures was a magic I learned there, and it has never left me. I had delighted in nourishing myself well as I started to enjoy exercise, and I still cherished sharing my cooking. When we were a new couple, D was working in London and would come down to Brighton every Friday night as soon as work would allow. The nervous anticipation of stirring a promised seafood risotto, sliding a pie into the oven as I got word that the train had passed Haywards Heath and laying out the starter I knew we both loved had barely had the time to become treasured memories. But as time passed, the pressure of 'really looking after ourselves' during the grind of the IVF had taken a little of the sparkle out of my joy of cooking. I would still read recipe books, devouring new writers and rereading old favourites as a way of winding down – a sort of culinary Sunday-night TV – but it had increasingly become tinged with guilt. Was I getting the right nutrients? Was I giving us the best chance of conception?

Should I sprinkle bee pollen on everything? Or spinach? And what about the oysters? The mackerel? The seeds?!

All that had changed now. As I headed into late pregnancy I had batch-cooked favourite meals for the freezer with the fervour of the British Military Catering Corps. Freezer bags full of Leon's famous meatballs. Nigel Slater's green chicken curry. The bespoke, pimped-up Delia Smith lasagne that I had been perfecting since university. Nigella's chicken shawarma. Felicity Cloake's pies. Divertimenti's tray bakes, from a recipe hand-written for me by the café's chef over a decade earlier.

Since L had been born I had barely stopped eating, pre-occupied by a permanent search for that one special meal which would make everything better. If I could just choose and make the right dish, I told myself, we could sit down together at last and I could truly have my husband's attention, if not devotion. I would try ever more elaborate recipes and menus, desperate to recapture that long-forgotten mood that would bring us together again. I began recreating old favourites: a paella we had once had on New Year's Eve, a steak cooked the way we had enjoyed it on an early anniversary, a carbonara to the recipe we had had when visiting Italy while that embryo had been making itself cosy after all. Five-year-old shopping lists fluttering out from between pages closed for years, in the hope that they would cause the needle to skip on the record, and we could be back to the closeness we had shared in the past.

D and I sincerely did want each other to be happy, but we had lost our way on how to get there. We were stuck in a grim rut of snack-buying. One of us would buy the other something we knew they liked, but 'shouldn't' eat. That person would protest, but then seize the baton of reciprocal snack-buying for the next day. With each bag of Wotsits, popcorn or Minstrels my heart would sink, knowing I had nothing even close to the willpower required to leave them untouched. But that same heart would also skip a beat.

You remembered me, and you wanted me to be happy.

At the same time I became desperate to start weaning the baby. I had had to stop breastfeeding as the shingles eventually got the better of my milk supply, but I was equally keen to avoid using only formula and to get some healthy food into him. Repeated midwives had reminded me not to contravene the World Health Organization's guidelines by starting to wean before he hit six months old (after all, he was barely five months). Did I dare to overrule these authorities? Well, yes, I found it suddenly much easier when that very month the WHO announced Robert Mugabe as their new Goodwill Ambassador. It suddenly seemed more reasonable to follow instinct and take my own advice over theirs: it was time to wean.

Alive with the excitement of being released from behind the pump, I threw myself at the new challenge, experimenting with flavours, textures and colours, delighting in L's enthusiasm for the world of food. It seemed so simple, so blindingly obvious what he needed and he took it all with relish. I grew more and more confident at trying new things out on him with ever greater daring: parmesan, ginger, cinnamon, beetroot. I would present them all with a grin and he would match my smiles, reaching for more each time.

I grew resigned to D avoiding my gaze at home-time, and prepared myself to hand the baby over each evening, putting my headphones on and going to the kitchen to cook. I listened to audiobooks and podcasts as I spooned rainbow-coloured mush into carefully organised ice-cube trays, before starting on dinner for the grown-ups. Somehow, what was so obviously healthy for L didn't apply to me as I tried to quell the anxious knot in the pit of my stomach with snacks. Portion size remained what it had been during pregnancy and breastfeeding, and every bit of weight I had gained clung to me as if for protection. I could almost feel the blood pooling in my body as I got heavier, moved less and felt further from myself.

And I did nothing to change that. My wardrobe was full of clothes that no longer fitted me. I couldn't even pull my pyjama bottoms up over my thighs and took to sleeping in old trackies. I was constantly surprised by how much space I was taking up. Strangers would shift away from me on the bus as my sides spilled over onto their seat. My thighs bled where seams rubbed together as I walked. Bras no longer did up at the back.

I didn't enjoy how I looked or how my body felt, but nor did I want to be ashamed by this. I had, after all, just been through nearly two years of IVF, a horrible pregnancy and shingles. I had a right to be this size, and owed no one anything smaller. What felt like a step too far was to love this new body, as I was constantly encouraged to do by the now incessant wave of social media. I should be proud! I should be pouring ceaseless praise on my every curve! Take more photos! Show more flesh! Closer, closer to the camera! Show us how much you love yourself!

I didn't love my body. It was fine, but I didn't love it any more than I loved any other passing stranger on the street: because that was what it was, a stranger's body. I was living inside a total unknown and having to pretend to be them every day. One morning as I walked briskly out of the bedroom heading to the bathroom I felt a slash of pain across my chest only to discover that as my dressing gown had flared open I had caught my nipple on the door handle. My nipple! What the fuck was it doing down there at elbow height?

I still dreamed that I was the size I used to be, a me who fitted on bus seats. I couldn't – wouldn't? – adjust my reality to this new shape. Because although I had gained a huge amount of weight, it wasn't just the weight that was different. When I stopped breastfeeding huge handfuls of hair came out every time I brushed it. Often, the hair was smattered with flakes of now-dried up shingles blisters. Brushing hurt, and it repulsed me, but to not do it would have been even worse. It was one thing I could still do in the face of the total lack of control I felt. The pain in my joints if I tried to run. The panic in my chest if I tried to swim. That hard-won agency, which had not just taught me to believe that I could achieve anything but taught me to teach others that too, vanished.

D seemed largely un-fussed by these changes. Perhaps the weight gain was not that noticeable, I told myself. Or was it because D wasn't looking? Also, D sincerely wanted me to be happy whatever shape or size I was. 'If you want to change things, change them, I support you,' I would be told. 'But if you don't, or aren't feeling up to the job yet, then don't. Just be happy with who you are.'

But who was I? I had physically changed so much that even my iPhone classified me as two different people in its 'Faces' section: before-late-pregnancy me, and late-pregnancy-and-motherhood me. Perhaps that was it: if I were so different from the self who had existed before all this baby madness began, why should D be expected to respond to me the same way? After all, I told myself, it couldn't possibly be the case that D was the one who had changed.

Could it?

Gradually, as the last of the shingles virus left my system, I felt more sure than ever that despite the anxious frown from the GP who had given me my diagnosis, and the quiet texts from my mother and sister, no, I really wasn't depressed. I was sad. And perhaps *I* wasn't the cause of my unhappiness. Slowly, I turned my gaze away from my constant inquisition of myself and my responses, and back to D. Slowly, slowly the Möbius strip started to unfurl, the eternal churning beginning to form one coherent train of thought. Dare I follow it?

Of course, I would have been a fool not to have ever asked any questions about D's gender identity. I had expressed curiosity as a friend, and even more when we became a couple. I had even asked outright, while we were engaged, if transitioning was or ever would be an option. I can still see myself, remember the pale enamel milk pan I was holding, drying up in the corner of our seafront kitchen when I had said it. I was barely able to believe I was daring to ask something so personal, but I was utterly comfortable that I knew what the answer would be.

'Obviously I would support you if that's what you wanted. I would be right by your side. I just wouldn't want to be, well, your *wife*.'

D had leaned against the countertop and laughed at me. How bourgeois of me to think that colourful self-expression and the odd bit of asymmetrical neoprene might mean something so drastic! Why box people in?! What a silly overreaction, I had told myself as my head hit the pillow that night. The world was changing, we lived in Brighton for heaven's sake, there were thousands of ways to be a man! We moved on, drenched with as much love as ever. We had so much fun, we just had so much fun.

In the years that followed, the topic would come up from time to time, but quickly I would be told that it was a non-issue. And I respected that. For the first time I was in a relationship where I was grown up enough to accept that there are – and will for ever be – spaces in a loved one's head that you just don't have access to. For years I had tried to know boyfriends 'completely', as if there were some graduation-level understanding that could be attained for every human. I would stare intently on first meeting parents, I would listen to every childhood memory I was given, treating each one as a potential skeleton key, trying to attribute each specific family recollection to a present-day mood or behaviour. If I just paid enough attention, I would tell myself, I would crack it. But with D, things were different. Perhaps it was because I genuinely was more content in myself, surfing the gentle waves of success and self-acceptance that *Running Like a Girl* had brought me. And some of it must have been down to D's unquestioning, uncomplicated adoration of me. At last, if I didn't understand a passing mood or what lay behind it, I was happy to trust that from time to time we all drift off to those spaces in our heads to which no one is invited. At last, I wanted that for myself, rather than to be peeled open and examined like a fig fresh from the tree. So of course I would grant the same to my beloved. Thus, questions I might like to have pressed a little harder on, went unasked. And before long, things were further complicated by how easy it was for my queries to become smothered by the IVF and its myriad side effects. What was 'my' mood, and what was just the drugs?

'Have you plucked your eyebrows?' I once found myself asking.

I don't even remember the answer. It seemed so insignificant compared to the sharps box full of used needles next to my bed, the month's worth of scans I had booked up, eating into my writing time, and the impending egg-collection surgery a few weeks away. Was it tiredness, was it that *eyebrows* seemed like such a waste of conversation when you're both staring into the jaws of childlessness while trying to stay positive, or was it that it just didn't matter?

I will understand if you want me to produce a list of ever-mounting clues here. Something that would fit nicely into a TV drama adaptation about marital secrets, or a noisy tabloid headline for next time someone reveals an unconventional marriage. A trail of crumbs, which could have led me clearly to the truth. A piece of twine to follow to safety, out of this maze in which I found myself. But there was no pair of lace panties that I didn't recognise, no dress I suspected had been worn in my absence, no form filled in with an unfamiliar name. In the lives of flesh-and-blood humans I doubt that there ever is. Instead, there was a growing distance between us. Unsayable, but all-consuming. When we hugged – the only physical contact we now had – D's head was not buried in my shoulder where it used to be, but staring over it, eyes open, mind elsewhere.

The behaviours I was by now confronted with were not dog-eared pop-culture tropes about living a lie, but an increasing sense that my darling, darling husband – who had been with me through so much, and helped me to find the very best in myself when I had least expected it – was having some sort of breakdown and I was proving not just useless, but wilfully self-absorbed about it.

We had our beautiful baby. We could never have dreamed of a better, bonnier child. To be parents at all was beyond what we had let ourselves imagine but to be this besotted was bordering on outrageous. That D seemed to be unhappy was the glaring red flag that I could not ignore. Nothing – not the baby, not my cooking, not make-up nor hair nor infinite hugs – seemed able to shift the clouds that had now placed my beloved husband fully in shadow, and my heart feeling the chill of that shade.

Increasingly, I realised that keeping up any sort of normality was exhausting D. I would leave the room to make a cup of tea and return to an almost zombie-like presence, D staring out of the window with a face that looked close to cracking in desperation. But if I asked, if I *ever* asked, the response would ping back at me with a speed that left me breathless.

'I'm fine.' But this wasn't fine.

From time to time I would come home and see the damp evidence of half an hour ago's tears. Glistening eyelashes, the darkness of a wet sleeve, sniffs that were nothing to do with hay fever. But again, any enquiry was batted away even before the question was fully formed. I was left giddy by the velocity with which the mood could change from the all-consumingly matey hugs and early nights which seemed designed to avoid any sort of sincere goodnight kiss, let alone genuine intimacy, and full-beam adoration and treats for me and the baby (always a package, never just for me). Slowly, slowly, the pressure of being strong, being there, being normal for us was creating huge fissures in D, and the cracks – manifesting in mood swings, despair and a powerful sense of absence – were getting deeper. In turn, I was fast running out of responses. Compassion, resentment, neediness and frustration had got me nowhere in my search for a behaviour that might help us reconnect.

I might not have worried about any of those physical quirks, the apparent reaches for some sort of attention, if they had ever served to make D seem more content, to bring a greater sense of peace. But they never did. So, in the absence of either disclosure or further clues, I searched elsewhere for solutions. Was it drink? Surely I would have noticed? Was it depression? I asked, time and again. We had had therapy to combat the strain of the IVF, and I never felt we had been anything less than honest in that room. Now, I wasn't so sure.

For weeks I tried to get us exercising together. During our courtship we had often run side by side, even taking part in a half-marathon together. We undertook huge walks. D was at my side when I took my very first swim in Brighton's sea. We were not a couple who simply dreamed about our future, we were a couple who got on and *did* things together. Rarely had I felt more alive than when sweating alongside D, relishing a shared mission, whether it was an afternoon re-potting plants in the sunshine or a walk on the downs in the wind. Now, D was unpersuadable.

'Exercise is your thing.'

'If you want to get in shape, I'll look after the baby whenever you want.'

'I just need an early night.'

If I could ever have glimpsed that same smile, that same confidence which I had so strongly associated with our first years together, then none of this would have prompted such a crescendo of fretfulness in me. But I did not. There was no convincing D that I wanted us to do stuff *together*, that it wasn't about a race time or a path walked, but about a shared endeavour, spending time together out in the open. But no, D no longer seemed to want to be out in the open, with or without me. Slowly, it had ceased to be the tweaks to the exterior that were making my husband seem like a stranger. Now, it was the cavernous unknown within which was screaming for attention, and I could not cope. I had run out of Alexes to be. I did not have the strength to meet whatever storm was coming and survive. I could no longer be alongside someone who professed to love me but was visibly struggling to be loved by me.

Once, I had delighted in having a husband who embraced the feminine because their masculinity was strong enough to weather the storm of other people's gender expectations. But was that really who I had married? There was no one I dared whisper this to. There were no books, no websites or TV shows to guide me as I stumbled there, but eventually, after many months of confusion and avoidance, I was starting to wonder.

Was I actually married to someone whose masculinity could withstand a little flamboyance, or to someone embracing the feminine wherever possible because the masculinity they were born with distressed them?

Both of these potential husbands could have stood side by side in front of me, identical to a passer-by. The same hair, the same clothes, the same pose. The husband I had chosen, the man I had married, would have looked me in the eye and suggested going on a make-up mission together. It would have been exciting, thrilling even. A frisson of adventure after decades of tedium. But the other husband, the one I seemed now to be actually married to, was unable to stand and look at me eye to eye these days. And perhaps by this point there was only one reason why.

5

That autumn's murmurations on Brighton's West Pier were the most beautiful I had seen for years. Each evening at sunset the starlings performed their daily dance, sweeping and soaring around the derelict iron railings of the pier with a grace and urgency that made me sure they were dancing to the beat of my tattered heart. I began tracking sunset times and making sure I headed down each day, the baby and I bundled up ready to watch for the full hour of sunset. Him in his new winter anorak, the buggy propped up as high as it would go so he could see the birds up above. Me with my parka's hood up, a scarf covering most of my face against the wind. We snuggled together, mesmerised. He cooed, while I sobbed, still not quite able or not quite brave enough to confront the truth now roaring towards us: having finally had a moment to shift my gaze from myself, I could see clearly that I wasn't the only one in the household staring in the mirror, wondering where the body that I felt represented me actually was.

And at last, I could pinpoint the reason for the sadness. It was for a marriage that was now collapsing, and for a husband who was fading away in front of me like a photograph left in the sunny rays of my attention too long.

It wasn't just the question of D's increasingly complicated gender identity that was a preoccupation, but my response to it. I am straight. I can't just *become* gay any more than anyone gay can simply *will* themselves to be straight. And I was married. I had taken vows. Still, I was more sure than ever that this change, this turning in, this unhappiness oozing from D's every pore, was absolutely not a kick against the hyper-manliness required of early parenting, with all of its isolating standing-back-till-you-can-cut-the-cord, standing-back-while-the-wife-does-the-feeding, and standing-back-while-everyone-but-you-is-congratulated. D certainly wouldn't be the first husband to do something silly to grab attention after months of playing helper, but I had so much more faith in D's temperament, D's desire to love, D's essential goodness than that.

I truly loved D. I was wholeheartedly in love with D. Everything was better in so many ways since we had been sharing our lives, each of us adored by the other's family and looking forward for so long to starting our own. But I don't love women, not romantically. It mattered to me that I was married to a man. That had been my choice. But it had started to feel as though that choice was now being taken away from me.

It was undeniable. I could now see that over the last couple of years, with every tweak in appearance or language or behaviour, D had become more assertively feminine. That Möbius strip which my mind had been stuck looping round and round for so long was finally now lying at rest, fully unfurled. No longer did I wonder if it was as unjust to apply my preconceptions of masculinity onto my husband as it would be for D to have me adhere to some standard of femininity that had been cooked up over the years. I was starting to see that perhaps these nails were painted *in order to* express femininity, not *in spite of* it.

Each time I had told myself that it was 'just a phase', a quiet voice would pop up, wondering how different I was from the mother of a gay son who reassured her nervous self that he'd 'grow out of it'. This in turn left me in the position of having to accept that these new moods, this new self-expression, might be permanent. And if this were the case, what was I to do with my response to it?

Not my judgement, but my response. My instinctive, animal response. The quiver in a part of me I could never control, which had adored that slim line of hair running from belly button to crotch, but which had died the day that area was suddenly shaved clean. The heartbeat which had skipped at the very thought of lying in D's arms which now slowed at the thought that one day I might discover they had been shaved clean too. The flicker of desire which had curled deep inside when I looked at old – but relatively recent – photographs of our courtship, which no longer jumped at all when I was presented with this new husband.

Naturally people change over the course of a marriage. Would I turn my back if my husband put on weight, suffered an accident, or even aged differently than I had envisaged? Would I up sticks and try my luck elsewhere if the immediate masculine hotness of five years ago wasn't there? Of course not! We were soulmates, this was about more than just appearances. Could I, if this was where we were, still march on, smiling bravely? My hormones were probably still settling down, I had told myself. The magic might return soon, that *click*, it might not be so far away – after all, that's what all the blogs and the baby books say, I tried to tell myself.

But I knew we had wandered into territory far beyond those realms of blogs and baby books. The Insta-mums couldn't help me now. What I really felt like was the hero of a 1930s trashy romance novel. A gay man who dearly loved his wife and children, who enjoyed the stability of family life and its gentle rhythms. But one who, when the rest of the house was asleep, longed to lie in the arms of a man. To feel rough stubble when he kissed his beloved, holding a face cupped in his hands, to feel bulk rather than softness when pressed hip to hip, to stroke a firm slab of male chest rather than the forgiving cushion of a female one.

That was it: I longed to lie in the arms of a man. And I was increasingly convinced that I wasn't.

The sense of an incoming storm overwhelmed me. The air was getting heavier each time the three of us were at home together. I felt as if I were struggling to breathe in the mugginess around me, somehow taking in more moisture than air. Sound seemed almost muffled as the stormclouds seemed to hang lower and darker overhead. But instead of the excitement, the anticipation that I would feel before the onset of an actual storm – sleeping with the windows, or at least the curtains, open so I wouldn't miss it – I was consumed by dread.

Perhaps the worst of it was the crushing loneliness that accompanied these months. The baby was no longer a newborn; the stream of enthusiastic visitors had understandably dried up, but I wasn't working again yet either, just floating in the netherworld of the freelancer about to start things up once more. But the loneliness wasn't just practical: my marriage itself was a razed field of isolation.

The world is full of material – from sitcoms to literary memoirs to Instagram nuggets – about the peculiar loneliness of the new parent. Small hours spent awake, watching lights turn off on the street outside, listening to the foxes fight and fuck, waiting for that single tiny burp which will give you a chance of sleep. The specific effort required to reconnect with your spouse after childbirth is far from undocumented. But I knew my situation reached into worlds I barely dared to Google. There was nothing I had ever heard of beyond reality TV which represented a situation even close to mine. It is a dark day when Kris Kardashian seems relatable to you.

How to begin a conversation with a friend, a sister, a mother about what you think might be happening when you think it's . . . this? If I were overstepping the mark, I would be tainting my marriage for decades to come. There were countless occasions when I nearly spoke to friends about it, but each time I tried to compose a sentence, the words would jumble before they could reach my lips, as if I were taking a language exam at school, and was suddenly unable to remember how to ask for the way to the municipal swimming pool, just as I had done a hundred times before.

I didn't know anyone who had asked the questions I was now facing. I would edge around the topic, my breath would shorten, I was taking only tiny sips of air between sentences; and I would deflect with humour, or baby photographs, or pertinent questions about whoever I was with. How on earth to express this over coffee, or a cheeky Prosecco when a friend is simply expecting news on whether L was teething yet?

One Saturday in November I met an old school friend for a special day at the newly opened Thames Lido, and we had booked lunch and a swim. I was excited to have the chance to swim in an environment calmer than the sea, where I was still very unsure of myself, and because we hadn't seen each other in months. I spent the journey there rehearsing ways that I might discuss the panic chugging away at the back of my mind, delighted to be seeing someone I truly trusted. Then I reached poolside, and the mood was so light, so happy, that I knew I would say nothing. Why ruin her day? I told myself as my feet pressed against the tiled back wall of the pool and I pushed myself under. My hands parted in front of me and I watched the bubbles fizz past me as I forced air from my lungs.

You're still you, I heard myself say. *You've still got you.*

I reached the surface gasping.

There were a few of these meetings that autumn, times I nearly managed to articulate my situation to a few dear friends. But mostly I cried to the baby. The only consolation of him being big enough to want to face outwards from the buggy was that he would no longer see the tears trickling down my face: I would coo to him from above his head and he would be none the wiser.

And so by early November I finally found myself able to suggest to D that perhaps we needed help. Perhaps talking to someone else would be useful? I trod carefully, trying not to make any accusations that could make anything worse.

'You are so visibly unhappy,' I began, 'but you often seem to look for answers by changing things about your appearance instead of accepting who you are.'

A sad shrug.

'It's what's inside that matters, you must know that. You're wonderful, we both love you so much. I wish you could relax and enjoy that.'

And then came the answer.

'Yes, I do need to see someone. But . . . it's not because I can't, but because I *have* finally accepted who I am.'

'What do you mean?'

'I mean that I have accepted that I am not *this*.' That hand gesturing at the body I had lain next to each night for the last five years. 'I have accepted that this body doesn't represent who I *am*.'

I almost heard my world crack in two. I couldn't absorb what I was being told.

'It's because I have finally reconciled myself to who I am that I now see I need to change how I present myself to the world.'

A clap of thunder. The storm was finally breaking.

My marriage, which for so long had felt like sand shifting beneath me daily, gullying beneath my feet wherever I tried to stand steadily, was at last presenting me with a definite. After that first conversation, the seal was broken. Within a few days, interspersed with a couple of visits to a therapist to reassure me that I was in fact hearing what I thought I was hearing, the truth unravelled before me with breath-taking speed. My husband was a woman. My husband needed to transition. My marriage, as I understood it, was now unsustainable.

Quickly, so much about the last five years began slipping and refocusing as if an insistent thumb were rifling through the photo album of my recent history. Entire scenes had new filters put over them. Memories seemed to curl and warp like a miracle fish from a Christmas cracker. Panic, grief, despair, all crashing over me. But somewhere in there, already, a glistening shard of hope.

None of this was my fault. None of this had ever been anything to do with me.

All those hours spent distracted by worries, anxieties about doing the right thing, saying the right thing, feeling the right thing. And the distance between us had never been anything to do with my not having lost weight fast enough, not having breastfed well enough, not having tried hard enough at any of it. All of those shunned glances, turned shoulders as the lights went out, spurned attempts at intimacy. I now saw that they had been an attempt to conceal not affection, but feelings that D knew would spell the end of our marriage. All of that pain, all of that distance, had been a skewed attempt at preserving us, not a plan to destroy us.

With shocking immediacy, memories made me want to howl with grief for my two-years-ago self – shoe-shopping for our wedding, obliviously holding up hot pink Manolos and asking in all innocence, 'What do you think?' But other more recent memories made me want to leap sky high to celebrate my liberty.

Because I was free!

The truth was out and now I had been released from having to pretend that I didn't mind falling asleep in a woman's arms, that I hadn't noticed when my clothes had been admired, that I had never wondered if it was jealousy in those eyes every dogged time I had tried to breastfeed our tiny newborn.

It was never me. It had never been anything to do with me.

Suddenly, so much made sense. By being attentive, worried and communicative, I had effectively been a good enough partner to usher forward the end of the marriage. In a strange way, the very qualities that D had professed to desire in me as a wife were the same ones which had allowed us the space to reach for the truth.

The air up here in my new reality was sharp and mountain-clear. I was still sitting on the sofa, my hands on the knee of my beloved husband, but I was a thousand miles away. I was an explorer, staring down on territory I never even dreamed would exist. I was a climber, reaching heights I could never have imagined. I was a hot air balloonist, untethered and flying high above you all.

I had felt so sad for so long, my reality being presented to me again and again as other than it actually was. Time after time I had told myself it was my own closed-mindedness that was the problem, my lack of understanding, my self-absorption while my body was co-opted for others to deal with, to touch, examine, diagnose, fill and empty once more. Time and again I had been passive about what was going on with my own body, while worrying about D's. But now I had felt a rip, a tear and I was free.

This new altitude left me gasping. Yes, I was free, but I was also, while still on maternity leave, having to accept that my marriage was over. Just as the discussions around trans bodies, feminist politics and government policy concerning the Gender Recognition Act were reaching their most febrile, these same issues were clawing at my precious, hard-won little family.

Was I going to be a single mother? Would L have two mothers? Where would that leave me? Could I still be the 'main mother', or did D's change in status mean a reduction in mine? Who would help me with night-times? When did children learn pronouns? What would we live off, *where* would we live, what would life even mean from now on? Just as my future was starting to glitch with startling problems and questions, so the Kodachrome carousel of my past was turning faster and faster. Click, shift, click, shift, click, shift.

If this was who D was, who had I married? A hologram? Had any of that been real? Was I a fantasist? What did this mean about the fact that I was due in court in a couple of weeks? If I could imagine an entire marriage and produce a child with someone who turned out not to have truly been that person, what else could I be mistaken about?

We shared our usual bed that night, the room aching with emptiness as L enjoyed his new cot next door. The next morning I felt foggy, unsure if I was even remembering our conversation correctly. As dawn broke, I heard the familiar shuffle of movement outside the bedroom, and realised that the two of them were up. I stayed in bed and stared at the ceiling. It was ten years since my first book, a goofy guide to heartache, had been published. Back then, I thought I had seen it all. How scant my research had been, I thought, as the velvet darkness of the grief that comes with acceptance started to fold itself over me.

I rested my hand on the spongy flesh of my belly under the covers, pondering the sheer distaste I had felt for my body those last few months as it had let me down time and again. The fistfuls of hair in my hand, the pyjama bottoms that no longer reached over me, the tops that strained over my enormous, utterly defunct, breasts.

This? I thought. *You want to change yourself for access to this? How fucking dare you assume that this is better than how you live?*

The IVF with its endless needles and its confidence-crushing uncertainties, the doctors referring to my 'geriatric pregnancy' as they tried to keep the concern from their eyes, the hot, vengeful hand on my backside as I walked down the train carriage.

You want to throw everything away for access to this life, these treats?

I heard the baby cry. Life was going to carry on happening to me regardless of this change. The outside world wasn't going to care that I was seeing everything through an entirely new prism. Where a month ago I had been nervous about rebuilding my body, now I was presented with rebuilding my entire life.

There was no time to watch *Newsnight* or read vociferous columns about trans issues. I was going to have to navigate my way through this in real time, with real people. I would be aiming for a new body, a healthy, woman's body, with my husband doing the same. I had no experience to support me, no confidence left to boost me and no option to fail.

And before that, I had a court case to attend and Christmas to face.

*

The trial was set for three days before Christmas. Beforehand, a volunteer from the Witness Service had met me at the court. It was an appointment for vulnerable witnesses, its aim to show me the room itself. It is one of those services you don't know is available until you are in acute need of it, and I was hugely grateful it existed. A chink of light, a chink of humanity, a chink of foresight in a world that seemed so incomprehensible that winter. For months I had imagined the day of the trial, wondering about the layout of the court. How close to the defendant would I be? Near enough for him to notice my shaking hands? Within touching distance? Would eye contact be possible? Scenarios became real behind my closed eyes as I lay there in the dark, listening to the snuffles of my newborn as he fell asleep in a milky haze on my chest. I had wondered how this same body could have experienced that wretched conflict on the train as well as these oxytocin-hazed cuddles.

The day we visited the courts it was pouring with the sort of rain that a cinematographer might have deemed 'a little much' on seeing it in a script. Yet when we arrived at the sloping disabled entrance, hair in thick wet clumps around my shoulders, trainers sodden, baby screaming, a court official forbade me from using it as I hadn't filled in a form in advance. I duly lugged the baby and buggy up the twenty huge concrete steps at the front of the 1970s monolith, my heart already hammering with anxiety, close to bursting out of me by the time the court volunteer arrived. And when she did – a mild woman in perhaps her late sixties wearing a cardigan she had almost certainly knitted herself – I wanted to hug her for the gentleness of her voice alone.

She led me to a private room, one behind several doors which required key codes, and showed me to the vulnerable witnesses' entrance. My chest heaved with relief that I wouldn't have to arrive at that central reception again, running the risk of bumping into the defendant. But it chafed that I would have to creep in the side of the building: that doors were literally shutting for me because of his behaviour. We sat in this room, L on my lap letting out a subtle but consistent melody of tiny farts, and discussed how the day in court would be run. The volunteer briefed me to be prepared for a lot of waiting. She explained the order in which proceedings would happen, and then led me into the courtroom itself.

There was a lot of wood. An awful lot of bleached wood. My first thought was how much it looked like a sauna. My second was to start assessing who would sit where. I realised that I was shaking uncontrollably. The only other time I had shaken so violently was during a scan at one of my IVF appointments, when the nurse had accidentally tapped my vagus nerve, famous for being a hotspot in the nervous system which can instantly produce feelings of quivering and faintness. This time, the tapping had been psychological: out of nowhere my hands were trembling as if I were playing a jig on an invisible piano, and the edges of my lips became numb enough that I slurred when I asked to sit down.

The volunteer did not bat an eyelid but sat me down at the side of the room, L on my lap, clawing at my neckline for an ever closer cuddle.

'It's OK,' she said. 'It's natural. You will have thought about this a lot.'

'Yes,' I whispered, as I took the glass of water she had had the foresight to bring with her. I had barely had a second to think about the actual case yet it had been on my mind almost constantly. Suddenly the cumulative effect of this shadow that had been cast on things was juddering out of me as I sat there, soggy and shaken.

Once my trembling had stopped, we chatted a little about the seating in the court. She showed me the visitors' benches, where anyone could sit – my family, any press, or any friends of the defendant. I thought of those men, their shoes facing towards me as I stared at the floor of the moving train.

If that's what you feel happened to you . . .

It's not what I feel happened. It's what did happen . . .

Then the volunteer let me sit in the witness box, the baby on my lap, and showed me the choice of bible or secular affirmation. We discussed sight lines, how I would be able to see the defendant while I was speaking, and how he would be able to see me. As I sat there, twiddling with the buttons on L's cardigan, feeling the warmth of the turd he was gently releasing as he smiled up at me, I tried to imagine myself expressing clearly what the defendant had done to me that day. It wasn't the touch that had stayed with me, but its intention: to teach me a lesson for not being charmed by him. And the crumbling of my faith in people's goodness, at a time when I was already so physically vulnerable. My body still felt frail, lumpen, out of my control. Would I dare to speak out if something similar happened again?

But that court volunteer, her quiet manner which suggested she had seen the very depths of human nature as well as some of its most resilient survivors, went a significant way to counteracting those thoughts. The day of the case itself – and the days immediately preceding it – would have been so much harder if I had not had that visit to the court; and the kindness that woman showed me still buoys me up on random days when it seems like everyone is out to pay my invoices late, step in the path of my buggy or take that last seat on the train. She knew what I was going through; I felt it in every quietly held open door, every gentle turn of phrase, every silent nod as I babbled nervously about what to wear, how long the lunch break was, and whether it was Perspex or glass he would be sitting behind.

What led you here? I wondered to myself as we left. *What have you been through to spend your days showing this kindness? What have you seen?*

On the day of the case itself, though, she was nowhere to be found. I arrived with two heroic friends, both of whom were frantic with their own pre-Christmas family chaos. D, I decided, should look after the baby, who had thus far never been taken care of by a stranger. Today was not the day to start employing childcare. It had been explained to me that I had to sit through the entire trial including the defendant's evidence if I wanted to find out the verdict on the same day; the alternative was to wait to be informed via a letter after the Christmas break. With a friend flanking me on either side, the three magistrates – one woman, two men – entered and the trial began.

Various formalities were dealt with and announcements read out and then I was called upon to give my testimony. With sudden horror I realised that all the nights I'd spent visualising the day in court, even my wildest imaginings, could not have prepared me for the combative nature of being interviewed by a defence lawyer. The law had just been changed to prevent defendants representing themselves, so high was the number of cases in which women who had been victims of domestic violence were subjected to further emotional violence by their ex-partners in the name of 'questioning'. There had been a lot of back and forth for much of the autumn about who would question me, and eventually I had been told that it would be a lawyer. The cross-examination was brutal.

I am no longer sure what I imagined cross-examination would feel like, but I know I had never envisaged anything as ruthlessly personal. The immediate tack taken by the lawyer was that I was posh, or prissy, and that I simply didn't like the look of a drunk man with tattoos coming to sit next to me on a train. I was a prig who wanted to be left alone and when I wasn't, I lashed out in a way that could ruin a man's life. I was highly strung because I was pregnant and making jittery judgements out of hormone-driven fear. I was, by implication, wasting everyone's time because of my own petty prejudices.

When I had stood at Brighton station six months earlier, shaking with fear, I had thought that I was safe. Safe from the defendant, of course – he had been arrested, barely able to stand, the minute that he had left the train. But I also thought I was safe from being called a liar, being trapped, being held responsible for what speaking honestly could unleash.

I had been grabbed before. It isn't too much of a stretch to say that most women have felt a clammy paw on their backside at some point in a bar, an office or on public transport. And most of us know that that's as far as it will go: a metaphorical tap on the shoulder reminding us whose world we're living in, and how much rage is sitting there, ready to bubble over if we disagree. I didn't think I was about to be violently raped by that man. My overriding worry was that he was simply so unsteady that he might hit my baby bump. But what really terrified me was the response to my telling the truth, out loud in a crowded train, for my own safety. Those moments in that front train carriage, trapped by his friends, telling me I was a liar and that people in the carriage behind me were discussing how disgusting I was, had filled me with a cold terror that has stayed with me. The indignant confidence. The fury at my telling the truth. The reminder that I was vulnerable.

And here I was again, in the witness box, being told that it was the weakness of my character – my haste in judging someone who I simply didn't like the look of – that had led to us all being here. In any other year I might have acquiesced. I had spent most of the last couple of decades generally agreeing if someone told me I was wrong. It was only when I discovered running and then swimming that I developed any sense of strength, of confidence in myself. And even then, under pressure, I was still prone to go along with the consensus – particularly if the consensus was a man talking over me.

But it wasn't merely a case of the defendant having grabbed me that had led me to court that day: it was also my decision to press charges and pursue the case. Because in those moments at Brighton station, when I had believed I was safe, I had felt responsible not just for myself, but for every woman who had had this happen to her. That army of women who had been where I seemed to have spent so much of the last year: being told that their reality wasn't real, hadn't happened, wasn't theirs. That they had imagined a flirtation, that they had lied for attention, that they had fabricated for fun. I had read those stories as the #MeToo movement had taken flight, and I had realised how quick to judge I had been in the past. Not just to judge others, but to judge myself. I thought back to almost imperceptible brushes in boardrooms, to hands outstretched as I ran past in my trainers, to the Hollywood star I interviewed on the red carpet while his hand rested on my backside the entire time, knowing that because I was a lowly reporter I would get the interview rather than cause a fuss. For years I had willingly absorbed the idea that there must have been a part of me deserving that treatment, and that I would be better off ignoring it, working on my sassy clapbacks, focusing on the good guys.

I might have continued thinking this if it hadn't been for the heroic women (and others) who had spoken out that year, shifting my perspective on what was acceptable, and – crucially – making it glaringly obvious that I hadn't been alone in these moments. It had been happening every day, all over the world, and none of it was to do with sex. The very second I had felt that clammy palm on me I knew that sexual assault was nothing to do with sexual attraction, and everything to do with wielding invisible power.

That man had lurched into my space, and when I decided that the safety of my unborn child was my priority, he lashed out with a proprietorial grab to remind me that he could, if he chose, still harm me. I knew what flirtation felt like, I knew what a loving hand on my body felt like, and now I knew what the livid pulse of rage felt like.

But still I had hesitated when asked by the police if I wanted to pursue the matter. What point could there be? Why make a fuss when I was about to have such joy coming into my life? Wasn't it insulting to survivors of *real* sexual assaults to call my fleeting grab by the same name? But it was that army of women I felt around me which gave me the energy to say I would like to. I did it because I wanted the statistics recorded. I wanted the reality of my life, of our lives, to be a matter of recorded legal fact. I wanted men to stop feeling that a petulant impulse following an afternoon's drinking was an acceptable way to behave.

All those months later as I stood in that witness box, close to unravelling at the audacity of the defence lawyer's suggestions about my motive, my character and my state of mind, I thought again of those women. Of you. Of us. I absorbed the shock and called to mind the many women who had stood in similar positions – in far worse situations than my own. The women who had been caused pain, who had known their assailants, who did not have the confidence, support network or instinct for self-expression that I do.

No, I wasn't – as was suggested – fabricating a vendetta because I disliked a man's tattoos. No, my inch-thick handbag strap could not – as was put to me – have reached up and under my backside to feel like a warm human hand. No, I wasn't – as it was argued – too tired that day to know what was happening. I was sexually assaulted.

The Crown Prosecution Service defines Sexual Assault as when someone 'touches another person sexually without their consent', and because the grab had been on what is defined as a 'sexual area', that is what the defendant was charged with. But even that felt like rubbing salt into the wound. Having to stand up in a public space and have my backside repeatedly discussed in a sexual context riled me and undermined me. My arse is for sitting on, that day almost more than any other. And it wasn't just my arse that he had grabbed, it was me. It was *me.* He had grabbed my body, my self-worth, my concern for my unborn baby and my sense of independence in a world that already seemed fragile. All of it, he grabbed all of it.

Despite that time in the witness box, how ragged it left me and how I can still shake with rage when I recall it, I don't regret a second. Because I know I was right. And one of the reasons I know I was right was because that independent witness – the woman I did not even know was on board the train – had stayed true to her word, and after speaking to the police at Brighton station she had gone on record to confirm that she had seen it all happen. And she was prepared to come down to Brighton from Nottingham just a few days before Christmas to confirm the veracity of my story. I never spoke to her, beyond mouthing 'thank you' at her when she left the witness box, but I think of her too when I need to be reminded of people's intrinsic goodness.

And yet. Despite an independent witness, despite my sobriety on that journey, and despite the defendant having admitted to having drunk ten pints, ten gin and tonics, and two bottles of wine that afternoon, his version of events was deemed the more credible, and the verdict was Not Guilty. As the magistrate summed up how he had reached his conclusion, he explained that to be found Guilty would have a huge impact on the defendant's life. And that while he was sure I intended to be a reliable witness, there was a very real possibility that as I was pregnant, I must have been in a heightened emotional state and could not therefore be relied upon to give an accurate account of what had happened. Yes, it seemed my pregnancy rendered me more unreliable than his afternoon of not insignificant drinking.

When, a few hours later, I turned on my phone, I saw that I had been tagged into a photograph on Instagram. A woman called Wendy Altschuler had taken a picture of a Post-it note stuck into a copy of *Running Like a Girl* in a library in Arlington Heights, Illinois, explaining that a previous reader had filled the book with such notes containing quotes from the book as a random act of kindness for future readers. Wendy's post quoted this extract:

'*I wasn't a failure. I wasn't pathetic. I wasn't weak. I had proved that I could set a goal and meet it. I had shown that I could redefine who I was and who I could be. And I had discovered that tenacity in myself along with a huge well of goodwill in my friends and loved ones.*'

There I was, five years before, discovering these things about myself. Now it was in Illinois, as a random act of kindness for a total stranger. In that moment, I felt convinced that telling the truth – despite the devastation it had caused me – was the only path that I could reasonably have taken. Not simply telling the immediate truth in the face of a liar who had claimed not to have touched me. *But living truthfully.*

After all, wasn't the mess that D and I now found ourselves in a result of not being able to tell the truth, when it mattered most? And must that defendant not have made many harmful internal contortions to reach a point where he could stand up in court and lie? Did he not seem like a man in pain? And was it not my responsibility – more than my responsibility, my only route out of this – to live truthfully every day from now on?

I could no longer bear the weight of pretending.

From now on, I was in an LGBT+ family. We would always be different, and there would always be challenges. But for every person I avoided eye contact with, or told a sanitised, easier to process version of the truth to, I would be doing a disservice to us all. If those words on that Post-it, '*I could redefine who I was and who I could be*', written five years before in the gorgeous heat of falling in love with D, could come back and support me when I needed them most, then there could be no doubt that to live truthfully was the only path I could take.

For the first time, I felt a glimmer of hope that what we had done was the right thing. After all, it was my openness, my sincere and ongoing concern for D, and my lack of judgement about the multitude of ways a person can identify, which had created the space in which D had finally been able to speak the truth about herself. About who she really was. Sure, it had come at the expense of my marriage, but it was becoming clear that this spirit of openness was the only viable means of survival for the long-term health of this little family.

For so long I had felt disjointed from the 'club' that early motherhood so often seemed to be. The temerity of women who complained about problems I longed to have! The number of times I saw '*Don't worry, it's very common, it happens to everyone*' written in books, blogs and leaflets without a second's thought for the multitude of ways there were to be a mother. The casual assumption that every 'mum' had an accompanying 'dad'. As I felt the parameters of what a family could be urgently being redrawn, I considered all the new decisions our family would have to make – and I realised that perhaps it might not all be bad. Just as meeting D had turned up the colour in my world, the end of our romance was again presenting life to me through a different lens.

The one consolation of that court case had been the overwhelming sense of solidarity I now felt with so many women. Having taken the decision early on to keep it very private, I then decided that writing something about the case might be appropriate. I reposted that image I had been tagged in, writing a caption in a few breathy seconds before I could talk myself out of it.

> I have never needed to see anything more. Today I finally went to court to give evidence in the sexual assault case from March this year. From the moment I contacted the BTP to the Witness Support Service ladies who looked after me today, I was so heartened by how there were proper systems in place and I was protected and respected. The prosecuting lawyer was amazing, and let me know that I was believed. But the defendant was found not guilty. The magistrate said that while I was a reliable witness I 'must just have made a mistake'. I didn't make a mistake. I know what happened. I know where his hand was. And I will know for the rest of my life, as will he.
>
> But the thought that somewhere on the other side

> of the world, someone is bothering to make sticky notes of my words just to be kind to total strangers is more consoling that you will ever know. xxx

It was extraordinary what warmth and consolation rushed my way as a result. By sharing, I had found solace. By connecting, I had eased stigma. Now, it seemed clearer than ever: I had to do it all over again, but on a bigger scale, and for the well-being of my son as well as myself.

As I stood in the queue at our local bakery the next day, 23 December, I felt a tap on my shoulder. I turned around to see a woman in jeans and a jumper. She looked like a busy mum, someone who could have walked past me in my neighbourhood a hundred times.

She smiled and said, 'I saw your post about the assault, it has happened to me too. Thank you for telling the truth.' We hugged each other, both holding back tears. But the clouds were lifting a little. The darkest day had already passed.

Bracing yourself to accept the judgement of others leaves you stiff-shouldered, aching and brittle. I couldn't avoid the truth of what had happened to my marriage: we were going to separate, even if practicalities meant it couldn't happen immediately. The decision was regretful, heavy with heartache on both our parts; but it was impossible to make me lesbian, just as it was to stop D from being trans. The terms under which I had entered the marriage had altered too much for us to be sustainable as a couple. D and I were both desperate to remain a family, for there to be as little change as possible for L, to keep supporting each other as best we could. Despite the specks of hope I had seen, however, I was realising that I was, for now at least, in a state of grief-stricken shock, barely able to articulate my feelings except to those closest to me.

Explaining the fragility of the situation to others was difficult. I would try to be brief – to disclose quickly but discreetly that we had separated, to try and avoid any allocation of blame – but then found myself having to politely bat away people's assumptions about the sort of 'man' who would leave both wife and baby at such an age. Then, I'd find myself stuck. Where to begin? To tar D with having 'left' us wasn't fair on anyone, but I didn't want people to misunderstand my actions, to reach the conclusion that it was me who had somehow tired of my husband the minute I had got my baby.

On top of having so many of my decisions about early parenthood whipped away, I often found myself duty-bound to explain or justify D's decisions – in so far as they were decisions. People called to check if I was OK; they had sensed that things had changed, that I had been quiet. They deserved an explanation but often I didn't feel like giving one. I didn't want sympathy from people who thought it appropriate to give me their opinions on gender politics, when what I wanted was to work out what my own were. I couldn't lose myself in a morass of resentment and bitterness, but nor could I become a full-time spokesperson for someone whose decisions were so personal.

I was often defensive on D's behalf. It was clear that being trans had never been a choice so much as an essential part of her reality, and I had spoken to enough friends about the torture of coming out to know that to some degree it wasn't my news to discuss. Yet it *was* my life which had borne this huge burden. It was tricky to be caught in a hamster wheel of mini gender-studies classes, repeatedly explaining emotions that essentially weren't my own. Each time, each person, each interaction, required a fresh – hastily made – set of decisions about how far to explain, how long to spend, how much of another precious day of my baby's infancy I wanted to spend mired in this.

The huge asset I did have was something I thought I had long ago lost: my choices, my agency, my response to the situation. Since we had begun the process of IVF and I had effectively handed over my body, I had felt those choices, that sense of agency, removed time and time again. Just as I had sat behind a breast pump, and in a courtroom, and watched with trepidation as my husband had tried to express feelings that none of us really have adequate language for yet. Each time, I had felt myself experiencing things as a bystander rather than a participant. Each time, I had felt my part in the story brushed away as the bigger players in the narrative made their moves. And each time, the narrative had not quite reflected my truth, as I wandered, groggily, in a maze of half-truths, medical mishaps and outright lies, gripping on to reality by my fingernails, unsure what was up and what was down. Now I had the biggest choice of all – how I was going to react.

My response would become my story.

But first, I needed to understand what was anger at my situation, what was anger at my own body and how I currently felt about it, and what was political anger, raging at a world where admitting who you really were could still be so terrifying.

I had to be curious about how we had got here, and why it was hurting so much. Not just the separation, but how two people who genuinely loved each other so much could have got so far without these basic truths becoming obvious. And why my responses had been the way they were. What was my own relationship with my body, and where had it come from? I needed to look back, to try and work out which 'me' from my past I was going to try to resurrect, and why.

6

When I stopped growing, a year or so before I took my A levels, I developed mysterious and debilitating pains in my limbs.

For years I had had intermittent but furious bouts of pain. At first, I had no idea what was happening to me. My knees and hips would be seized by soul-sapping agony as if my joints were both being clenched and stretched, somehow simultaneously. 'Growing pains,' my grandmother told me one summer holiday, when I lay on the beach in Cornwall. A rare sunny day at the seaside was wasted as I clutched my knees to my chest and rocked back and forth on my towel, sand spraying, face wincing, temper fraying.

Growing pains were surely a wartime foible, long left behind by the wonders of late twentieth-century science. How could something as universal as *growing* hurt so much? When the pain passed, it was instantly forgotten, but a few nights later I would be woken again by a furious grating sensation as my femur seemed to be reaching to escape from my hip socket, yearning for freedom as I slept. On it went, month after month. I never quite knew where or when I would be gripped next, which part of me the pain would strike, or how long it would last.

Eventually, in older adolescence, it passed. The pain – and associated anxiety about it recurring – that had dogged me for years melted away like snow under wintry midday sunshine, and my body seemed to have made peace with itself. How wrong I was. In fact, the growing pains had been a mere opening act.

At first, I was distracted by the appearance of my breasts and hips, believing them to be the culprits behind my teenage blundering. I had always been awkward, but now I was becoming laughably clumsy. I could no longer turn the corner out of a room without catching my new hips on the edge of a table, a bookshelf, a desk. I tried to slide between display stands in a department store and left make-up and hair clips scattered in my wake. Crockery was rarely safe on a table I was sitting at. Playing the goofball was my only defence mechanism. It was useless against the mayhem, but stemmed the worst of the laughter.

Then came a fresh wave of pain. Still growing pains, but of a very different kind. The growing in my bones had stopped but not, it turned out, in my ligaments. My wrists would throb within half an hour of writing, my ankles would be sore after walking between classrooms. My hips and knees were not as bad as they had been, the grinding ache had shifted outwards to my wrists and ankles. I would curl up at night, grasping each wrist in the opposite hand as if giving myself a Heimlich manoeuvre, and wake up in the same position, the pain having barely shifted.

Now the worst of the pain was specifically brought on by writing. It was just as unavoidable as the hip pain: this was a time before mobile phones, an era in which the ability to pass notes in class was the ability to maintain friendships. The margins of all exercise books were filled with snark about teachers' hair, details of boys currently under scrutiny, and analysis of period pains, breast growth and general self-maintenance, all of which were topics of vital importance if I were to keep up with the ever flowing rapids of a teenage girl's friendship circle. Without the ability to scribble at speed, potentially while nodding at a whiteboard and feigning great interest in quadratic equations, I would be an outcast. So I took the pain. I swallowed it again and again, until writing an essay made me weep, wrists gripped and pinched by vice-like agony the minute I put my pen down.

Would a mobile phone have been any better? I suspect not: a sore thumb and uneven shoulders would probably have hurt just as much. These days, I have reverted to using a fountain pen for all of my note-taking. I write slowly and deliberately, forcing myself to think about what I'm saying, thinking, planning. I enjoy committing to handwritten thank-you notes for my friends, and choose both pens and ink with great precision. The years I spent gripping a Bic biro until I had finished my train of thought haunt me every time I write a shopping list. Teenage me, clinging tighter and tighter to the plastic edges as the callus on my middle finger grew rougher, knowing that the second I let go the throbbing would begin, is always there, still hovering as I sign contracts, doodle for my son, and tinker with my daily to-do list.

Back then, doctors didn't really know what to do with me. I visited endless specialists, I had CT scans, I was taken out of classes to have strange lasers pointed at my wrists in an attempt to ease things, but nothing was able to compete with the sheer volume of handwriting I was having to do: it was my final year of A levels and I was doing three and a half arts subjects. Even if I had stopped gossipy note-writing, the legitimate notes I now took in class were endless and the number of essays set seemed infinite. My sleep was scrappy, and my only solace was reading, sitting very still, trying to focus on the words in front of me until the throb-throb-throb of my wrists eventually dissipated a little.

Exams loomed ever closer, while a proper diagnosis seemed ever further from my grasp. My imagination was dancing, filled with the stories, authors and ideas we were studying. Aeneas frolicked alongside Lady Chatterley across Hardy's Wessex, tales spanning generations interweaving while my ability to express anything about how I felt or what I thought about them was stymied by the physical pain. What was the point in knowing about Dido being dumped by Aeneas if you couldn't pass notes comparing what Aeneas might look like in the movie adaptation of your imagination? Or to compare Dido's romantic travails to classroom romances of your own? Why even familiarise yourself with *Far From the Madding Crowd* if not to engage in half an A4 pad's worth of debate about whether Gabriel Oak or Sergeant Troy were hotter?

A joy in writing was emerging, but with each step forward came an accompanying wince of physical payback. A laptop was an unimaginable extravagance; no one I knew even had one let alone considered it appropriate for school. Patience was the only solution. Write slowly, wait, write a little more, try to rest well, and repeat. Patiently, exactly how every seventeen-year-old girl wants to live.

Eventually paperwork was signed allowing me to have extra time during my exams, so that I could rest my wrist every half-hour or so. It did little to help, though, only serving to extend my time in the exam room without any real respite from the pain. I sat in the back of the school hall alone, so that when the others filed out of the exam they wouldn't pass me or be able to make any eye contact. I scrawled on, clenching and unclenching my fists in the hope that it would release the intensity of the ache, but it never did.

Two months later there was the phone call to the school office to receive my exams results: I had not got the grades I needed for the place I had been offered at the University of Cambridge. That August afternoon, it felt as if the door to a new world was being slammed shut, and in part because of my physical limitations. I would no longer be off to read Classics in six weeks' time, independent in body and mind. Instead, I would be living with my parents, on the boring military barracks in Germany where my dad was then posted, while my friends travelled the world or at least engaged with its adult mysteries on campuses up and down the UK. My father came home from work with an enormous bunch of flowers for me, and an even bigger hug. We headed to the (immaculate) local outdoor pool where I cried in the water, tears hidden by the chlorinated depths. It felt as if every certainty I had about the world was ending. In fact, the world at large was just about to unfold itself before me for the very first time.

Circumstances meant I was stuck in the sterile surroundings of a post-war army camp. Rows of grey northern European buildings housing administration and accommodation for an army maintaining the dying embers of the Cold War. A parade square for practising formal marches – or more usually for parking cars that I wasn't allowed to drive, the German limit being eighteen years old. But also on the barracks was BMH (British Military Hospital) Iserlohn, a huge hospital which had been looking after soldiers since the 1930s. Serving members of the armed forces were treated there, but so were their families – and countless babies were born there, with birthdays often bunched together according to the leave dates that had been granted during conflicts in Northern Ireland or, later, the first Gulf War. In 1985 the hospital had closed for six years for an enormous refurbishment, and now it was beautifully equipped with staff from all over the world as well as state-of-the-art technology. During the Gulf War of 1990 to 1991, staff there worked alongside those of local German hospitals and Bundeswehr (Federal Defence Force) medical staff, in what was known as Operational Friendship.

So magnificent was my self-absorption at this age that I had failed to notice this hospital was there at all until it presented me with a double whammy of opportunity. I had a year on my hands before I could start the degree I had by now selected to take at the University of Bristol, so finding gainful employment was a priority. There were limited career options for a seventeen-year-old girl with no real life skills in a military base, but after a single interview I found myself one of the staff of cleaners looking after this pristine military hospital.

My hours were 7 a.m. to 3 p.m., and my responsibilities took me from ward to ward. As autumn drew closer I would wake each morning at 6.00, have a slice of toast and hop on my bike, riding across the barracks to the hospital basement where I would stash my coat and packed lunch, and begin a day wrestling with huge industrial floor polishers, monumental quantities of bleach, and endless cans of furniture polish.

After a year spent close to buckling under the pressure of exams, quivering with the threat of a university rejection, the repetitive nature of the cleaning job was a welcome relief. I quickly found out how to get the work done with minimal effort, thanks in no small part to the team of other cleaners – mostly soldiers' wives – who showed me the tricks of the trade, as well as the best quiet corners within the hospital for the rare sunny days when heading down to the basement to eat our sandwiches under the glare of strip lighting seemed just too bleak. We would have devoured whatever our Tupperware contained by about 11.30 a.m., reading the tabloids we borrowed from the closest waiting area. Nascent Britpop, Fred and Rose West, the recently published *A Brief History of Time*: we would grapple with all these and more as we flitted from hospital gossip to world affairs and back again, via insider secrets such as which were the better mops to use on new linoleum. There was none of the feverish tension of a gang of over-educated teenagers on the cusp of self-perceived greatness, but there was a lot of laughter. I loved every second, and it got even better when I found the room where they stored the old newspapers.

Ever the enthusiastic snoop, it was not long before I was diligently watching and listening out for all the drama that a hospital affords. I quickly learned where the most interesting doctors worked. Within a month a gynaecologist had taken me on a date – to Dortmund no less! – though all that came of it was a ride in an open-top Mazda MX5 and an early insight into mansplaining. But when I found the newspaper cupboard, everything changed.

I never found out who was doing it, and I had the good sense not to ask, but each week the supplements from the weekend papers were stashed in one of the cleaning cupboards on the psychiatric ward. Unlike other areas of the hospital, there were no inpatients on this floor, so it was perfectly possible to clock in for my shift at 7 a.m., head straight to that department, lock myself into the apparently-never-used disabled bathroom and spend the first two and a half hours of the day reading about topics as ludicrously diverse as Rachel Whiteread, Ian McShane and the apparently soon-to-be-a-big-deal Tony Blair.

Detached from the pressure of having to regurgitate the information in exam form, causing myself pain and anxiety, I devoured this eclectic primer in modern Britain. I followed my nose, starting to recognise names such as the Saatchi brothers, the Dust Brothers or the Menendez brothers. All information was suddenly rendered equal, uncategorised by academia, its only value whether reading about it was worth the risk of getting caught not working. This went on for months. Five thousand-word profiles of Martin Parr, an analysis of Daniel Day-Lewis's method acting, the columns of Zoë Heller and Helen Fielding, all chomped through with the same steady commitment as my lunchtime bag of Wotsits.

But while I was developing as an adult, learning to take risks, understand the art world and simply hold down a job, one thing remained resolutely the same: the pain. Sure, my wrists had been better since I had been able to stop the relentless writing, but they still ached most days, as did many of my joints. And the pain was still accompanied by its ever-present shadow, anxiety about the pain itself. What did it mean? Why could no one properly diagnose it? Would it ever end? Or simply get worse?

When it became clear that finishing my exams was not an end to the problem, my parents took me back to the GP, who in turn referred us to a specialist in the very same hospital I was then working in. Still a minor at seventeen years old, I was a military dependant and therefore entitled to care at BMH Iserlohn. So off I went.

Mr Nazra, a small, keen-eyed rheumatologist with round John Lennon glasses, thinning hair and an impeccable bedside manner, was the first medical professional to treat me as a patient in genuine pain, rather than a hysterical teenager who was prepared to keep upping the ante to avoid taking stressful exams. He was more used to seeing wounds inflicted either on the battlefield or in training in preparations for it, but he was not in the slightest bit irritated by a girl who said her hands hurt so much that she cried.

He asked me to do a series of stretches and bends: could my thumb touch my forearm? Could I bend my finger back more than ninety degrees? Could I bend my knees or elbows in the 'wrong' direction? He watched as I tried each feat, quietly and calmly walking around me and seeing how I moved. He also asked a series of questions about what I had been able to do as I was growing up. With what seemed like startling insight, his final enquiry was whether, 'As a child, you used to amuse your friends by contorting your body into strange shapes?'

How did he know? How had touching the floor with the palms of my hands opened a window allowing him to glimpse my technique of buffoonery to make up for my ridiculous clumsiness?

'Yes. Yes, I can do things like click my elbows out and make my little fingers look funny.'

Please, please, don't let this turn out to have been in my head all along, I thought as I gripped the arms of the chair and answered truthfully.

'I'm very bendy, and I'm very clumsy – that always makes people laugh too.'

The truth was out.

But Mr Nazra seemed not to find my problem complicated, or even silly: I was hypermobile. I had scored highly on what I now know was the Beighton test, which is used to assess whether people suffer from the disorder. It's not uncommon; it's often confused with other things, and it very often manifests just after a young adult has stopped growing. It means that the collagen in joints and ligaments is softer or stretchier than usual, causing joints to be less well held together than they should be, leading to strain, hence the pain. In my case, he explained, it looked as if when my body had stopped growing my ligaments had not, leaving them all a little too loose for the me that they were supposed to be holding together. Overworked by the effort of keeping my flailing body – totally unused to any real exercise after years of avoiding competitive school sports – in one piece, they were almost literally buckling under the pressure.

I was awestruck that there was such a simple explanation, and fascinated at how straightforward Mr Nazra seemed to find the situation. In hindsight, it seems perfectly clear that the shift was not in the problem, but perhaps in how I presented to the professional I was seeing out of school uniform, with exams no longer the main source of pain, it now seems obvious that I seemed calmer, more reasonable, more *reliable.* But what was to be done? Was there even a solution?

'It's very simple,' Mr Nazra explained. 'You have to strengthen your muscles in order to have them help your ligaments. You need to balance yourself to find your strength.'

I stared blankly, unsure what he meant by this.

'Where do you live?' he asked, aware that patients were referred to this state-of-the-art hospital from any number of army bases in Germany.

'Here, in Iserlohn,' I replied.

'Well, that's perfect, my dear.'

I blinked.

'I am going to send you to our physical rehabilitation clinic!' he said with a smile. I winced.

I knew what the rehabilitation clinic was: I had seen the patients working out in the parade square, and I knew that there was a gym. This unit at the hospital was large, for physical recovery for soldiers injured in or out of battle. Whether they'd fallen down the stairs after a night out or fallen in the heat of conflict, all serving soldiers needed to be, quite literally, fighting fit. The unit was renowned for being well staffed, filled with new equipment and usually full of men with dramatic injuries, particularly from the recent Iraq conflict. But at the moment it turned out that they had a space. And I, a seventeen-year-old girl, was about to be admitted to it.

'But . . . it's for the soldiers,' I protested, grimly remembering grassy-kneed press-ups on chilly lacrosse pitches.

'Yes, but you are entitled to be treated there as well. And it's a wonderful opportunity!' Mr Nazra smiled. 'I am sure that if we work on these muscles, you will have some peace from the pain.'

Fresh out of school and still smarting from the humiliation of not getting the grades I had hoped for, I quietly submitted to the voice of authority. The twofold shock of being diagnosed and then being prescribed 'sport' left me with mixed feelings. On the one hand, there was a simmering sense of celebration at having avoided the worst-case scenario – a life of infinite physical pain ahead of me – that had been my darkest fear. On the other, exercise as a solution had never crossed my mind, and now I was having to confront it head on. I sat staring out of the window at the parade square while Mr Nazra filled out the relevant paperwork. I was to begin my physical rehabilitation in ten days' time. I would be an outpatient, and as long as I was committed to riding my bicycle to and from the hospital, I would 'only' have to attend three to four hours per day of treatment. However, I would be on site for most of the working day, allowing for lunch and breaks between exercise.

Since abandoning the childhood frolicking of my pre-teen years, I had only ever taken exercise under duress, encased in old-fashioned school uniform, including short pleated skirts for lacrosse, my modesty kept in check by huge navy knickers woven from impenetrable navy cotton and worn over our regular knickers. I owned nothing I could wear for a day of what my mum's Jane Fonda LPs suggested was called 'working out'. The selection of clothing in the local NAAFI store was not, as we'd say now, motivational, so I had to head to the local department store, Karstadt.

Because of my cleaning job, and the fact that my parents were not charging me any rent, I had what felt like an unusually large amount of money to spend on my new workout wardrobe. Thus far, I had only used my new-found fortune to buy checked flannel shirts as close to Alicia Silverstone's Aerosmith video 'look' as I could find, and Prince CDs. Yes, I was saving to go travelling, but it seemed reasonable to dip into my funds if I were going to be wearing sports kit all day every day for two months. Two months!

But it was the early nineties and sportswear was at that point only worn for going to raves. Adidas trainers weren't the ergonomic running machines that they are now, they were simply flat Gazelles for standing around listening to Jamiroquai or the Brand New Heavies in. And Nike was just a logo I sometimes saw when the Olympics was on TV. My dad, by now past the heyday of his marathon mania, only ever wore Ron Hill, with New Balance on his feet.

So I bought myself a few pairs of cycling shorts-length shorts, some baggy T-shirts, some crop tops and some, um, workout onesies? I have no idea what today's athleisure market would describe the garments as, but they were not dissimilar to a weightlifter's outfit. The shorts were very short, and attached to a flesh-skimming vest top. And that was how I turned up for day one of physical rehabilitation: clueless and shrinkwrapped in Lycra.

The most exercise I had done over the preceding two years was a little running or swimming. The swimming would be slow, thoughtful breaststroke in the school's indoor pool. I had no idea how to put my head in the water and do front crawl, and I had no intention of trying to work it out. Instead, I used the echoey calm of the pool – a sanctuary far removed from the frenzy of the lacrosse pitches – to stretch body and mind, ticking off slow lengths as I daydreamed through the water.

Running was something I would do in bursts, with one goal in mind: weight loss. I would wake early, wriggle into my big blue pants, and give myself a hypercritical appraisal in the bedroom mirror, before creeping out and legging it up and down the fields for half an hour listening to Deee-Lite on my Walkman. There was no strategy: the sport taught at school was purely competitive. No heed was given to what was healthy, what might clear our minds or benefit either our muscular or cardiovascular systems. Our team games – lacrosse, tennis, athletics – were solely about winning. They took priority and I avoided them at all costs.

Would I have listened if we had been educated about fitness or mental health rather than mere victory? I doubt it. Because a larger lesson was already being learned, and more thoroughly: thin is best. You are both not enough and too much. It was there in the magazines we devoured, the music videos we would pounce on, the front pages of every tabloid we passed as we entered the newsagent for a stealthy packet of sweets.

Sure, there was no social media, no rolling celebrity news, no cameraphone in every back pocket, but there were also no alternative voices. Thin was best, and there was no other narrative. There were no blogs, no Google searches, no TV channels beyond the four terrestrial ones. And – God forbid! – there was no suggestion that our bodies were there for our pleasure, or indeed that they were our bodies at all.

We had our mothers, our media and our teachers. And while I hope (and in some cases suspect) that our teachers had wild and colourful interior lives, filled with vivacity and love, we never saw it. The very suggestion of it was forbidden. As was the idea that these women might have a physical life. We never saw them exercise, we never saw them dance, and we rarely saw them smile. In most cases there was never a hint of any sort of partner. Any advice or pep talk was given entirely in this context, and the suggestion was that in order to be good, or to do well, we would be best off following their lead. Because that way safety lay.

These suggestions were not made without care. They did want us to be safe. But they wanted us to be safe at the expense of teaching us anything valuable about discovering life and all its trifle-sweet layers of excitement and romance with either others or ourselves. Our biology teacher was a middle-aged man whose small fish badge on his lapel suggested that he held a strong Christian faith. This was supported by his dogged manner of prefacing any discussion of reproduction with, 'When a man and a woman fall in love and get married and decide that they want to have a baby . . .' The idea that sex might have existed beyond that set-up was closed down immediately. No further discussion, girls.

Of course, we were teenagers, we laughed it off and immediately spent the lessons passing notes about someone two years above us who had given a boy a blow job. But this attitude was genuinely harmful: we were never taught that we had a right to ask for sex to be enjoyable rather than 'successful'. We weren't taught how to keep ourselves safe in the world beyond the school's barbed-wire fence. Or that we were allowed to say no to someone even if we had been thinking yes two hours ago – before they started clawing at our bra straps. And of course we weren't told that we could pleasure our bodies all by ourselves, after lights out.

So when I stood there in my navy blue pants, appraising my teenage backside, it didn't cross my mind that going for a run might help me in other ways. That realisation was decades away. I just wanted a smaller bum because I had received the message loud and clear that a pert behind would increase my power. Not my power to get a good job, achieve self-sufficiency or effect worthwhile change in lives beyond mine – but that it would increase my sexual currency, which was the essence of where a young woman's power lay. So when after three or four days of erratic jogging my bum did not look like someone else's entirely, I assumed I was 'doing it wrong' and gave up. Thus, exercise had receded into the distance just as exams had loomed closer. My heart swells with melancholy when I think how the two of us could have helped each other.

When I arrived at the hospital's rehabilitation unit on my first day, I was more than a little wary about what the next couple of months might hold. The very reason I was able to receive this treatment was because I was young enough to qualify as my father's dependant, but the fact that I was legally a child was recognised in no way by the military physiotherapists who treated me as one of the soldiers from the minute I arrived. From that first fitness test – which I took in public, alongside several men, some decades older than me – I was treated as equal to the rest of the soldiers. If anything, I was expected to work harder. Given that you are able to join the army aged sixteen, perhaps they simply thought that I *was* one of the serving forces.

Whatever they thought of me, the staff in that rehabilitation unit really did play a formative part in my discovery of my own body. What is curious to me now is that I don't remember being treated as a girl, or even a woman at all. Could they really all have ignored this kid in their midst? Were they protective of me and kind enough not to let me feel patronised? Did I just get exceptionally lucky and spend two months in a unit where every single person treated me with respect? And what does it say that I find it extraordinary that no one placed a finger on me during those eight weeks?

The first few hours were a chance for the sports therapists to look over their new recruits, assess our fitness, and create a plan for 'recovery'. I flinched each time the word was used. What was I recovering from? Myself? The other twenty-five soldiers on the unit were genuinely getting over serious injuries, including one who had been crushed by a tank. All the evidence suggested that *I* was my own injury.

One of the first exercises we undertook was a classic 'beep test' on the hospital's small central quad. We had to run back and forth to the point of exhaustion, constantly trying to beat a series of ever closer-together beeps from the whistle being blown by the head of the department, a short, muscular man in military shorts and T-shirt, who seemed averse to smiling as a form of encouragement. Things have now changed, but for decades this simple beep test was one of the very cornerstones of British Military Fitness.

Once my basic fitness had been established, there was a series of bends, stretches, lifts and leaps to be made while further details were scribbled into the head therapist's notes. After a while, my programme was explained to me. Mornings would be an hour of circuit training in the main gym, followed by a group sport such as basketball, also indoors. After lunch, we would spend an hour on individual physio work for whatever our injury was, before an hour of further work in the swimming pool. Because each of these activities would be putting the body under quite a lot of strain, they would be punctuated by rest periods throughout the day.

In short, I was put on the sort of training regime that we now hear about actors undertaking in order to prepare for particularly gruelling roles. The only difference was nutrition, which was not mentioned once. There was no talk of protein to help develop the muscles that my programme was designed to help me grow. Nothing about any additional carbohydrates to give me the extra energy to undertake four hours of fitness a day. And there was certainly no discussion about supplements. As I was understandably too tired to cycle home for lunch, I did what my fellow soldiers did and I ate what they ate. Within a fortnight I was spending break time troughing two Yorkie bars and a pint of milk from the carton, while watching Jim Davidson video tapes in the common room.

The nineties were not a time for a holistic approach to physical and mental health. We were still a good five or six years off Madonna debuting her yoga-buff arms and suggesting that lifting weights might not be the only answer. And we were decades from the idea that exercise should perhaps include at least an element of psychological insight. We were there to work out and get better, where 'getting better' was seen purely as a matter of bone, muscle and sweat.

The strange context of this programme aside, it worked. I was so recently emerged from the A-level chrysalis in which I had been living for so long that I simply accepted the exercises I was given as another rule to follow. The routine, the uniformity of the days, the idea that grown-ups knew best how to make me 'better' were already ingrained in me. I swallowed the regime whole, and I loved it. Day after day I would turn up for circuit training, weights, basketball and swimming and slowly my body started to feel more like something that might work with me, if not *for* me.

There were no other women there, so I was spared the toxic teenage propensity to compare myself to those around me. The only comparison I had was the level of pain I had been experiencing when I had begun versus the level now – and this in turn began to shift my perception of what pain might mean.

I had begun to accept my ligament pain the same way that I had done period cramps: a regular, unavoidable horror that would dog me indefinitely. Now, I accepted that the pain of having to exercise hard was simply part of my life. Every inch of my body would hurt, particularly after the morning circuits. But slowly I began to feel the difference in the type of pain:

this wasn't the sharp, urgent sensation of a body not managing itself properly. It was the deeper, duller ache of muscles having worked to their limit. I came to understand that in order for muscles to grow stronger, we had to effectively 'rip' them, again and again and again. I learned that muscles are composed of thread-like structures called myofibrils and sarcomeres, which are highly sensitive to the motor neurons telling us to contract in order to lift, push and lunge. To my delight, I learned that muscle growth actually takes place while we're at rest, as the muscle fibres we've 'damaged' while working out go through a cellular process of fusing together to form new myofibrils, which in turn increase in thickness and number. I learned that bodybuilders call this growth hypertrophy, a term coined in the 1940s by Dr Thomas L. DeLorme, who had himself been working with the rehabilitation of soldiers injured during the Second World War. Their pain must have been a world away from mine, but progressive overload was the answer to each.

I ached, but now I understood which muscles were aching, because I had been targeting them that day. Or because I knew which tendon groups they were supposed to be supporting. I ached because I had worked hard, and that felt very different from a pain coming at me from out of nowhere. My body began to change: something profound in its structural integrity shifted. Where I had carried the extra weight of exam-time comfort food, my muscles slackening with underuse as I studied late into the night, now it felt as if strings were being tightened behind my back. Once a faulty doll, I was now repaired. Where my wrists had felt limp, halos of pain sparkling around them, now I felt power emanating from these aches. I relished engaging a glute muscle as I stood from the sofa, I enjoyed the delicious pulse of a newly discovered lat as I reached for a plate from a high kitchen cupboard, I felt chest muscles beneath my breasts when I pushed open a door. Yes, this was pain, but not as I knew it. Beneath my curves, there was a new structure, and one supporting me rather than holding me back.

Even months later, the focused exercise was still helping me to feel better in all sorts of ways. I was in physical control of my body, but more than that, I felt that we were working together, not against each other. I tripped less, I wobbled less, I felt pain less. Yet I did not feel lesser. For the first time, my physical self had seemed to fill with power, with control. It was starting to seem like a friend rather than a liability; doors I had long assumed slammed shut were opening for me, and I loved it.

My body had been problematic, and I had sorted that. Luckily for me, solving the problem of the pain had had the side effect of giving me what would be called 'a good body'. I was lean, not skinny. I had muscle definition all over, from the fronts of my thighs to my biceps, and the exact contours of a six-pack which rippled down my front. I looked like a Gladiator – not just a Roman one but, more pertinently, like one of the stars of the 1990s game show. My strength was visible. I was lambent, good health radiating from every pore. And people responded to it wherever I went, heaping far more praise on my physique than on the fact that months of sweat and obedience had given me a way out of crippling pain.

It was all, *Wow, you look amazing!* rather than, *I'm thrilled that you feel so much better.*

At the exact moment that I was at my most physically comfortable, I was also at my most outwardly pleasing. And this just happened to coincide with my heading to two of the most image-conscious cultures in the world. First up, I was heading to Trinidad and Tobago, and then I was going to spend the rest of my time until university in Italy.

7

Trinidad had long held a mythic quality in my imagination, only enhanced by the one visit we had made there when I was about ten years old. My mother had grown up there, the youngest of a family of five. Her father was of French extraction, who worked as an accountant on the island, and her mother had grown up in Bogotá, then Puerto Rico and Devon before ending up in Port of Spain and finding my grandfather. I had cousins my age who I had maintained feverish pen-pal relationships with, discussing everything from family gossip to the intricate details of our love lives. Each morsel of information I fed them represented several nights of agonising over whether I should share 'how far I had gone' with boys, lest the details should reach my uncle, aunts and thereby my mother. Now I was heading to the islands to 'play' carnival, which was taking place that year on my eighteenth birthday. The thought of an entire month out of my precious year between school and university, spent with them in the sunshine, sharing confidences and preparing for carnival, was intoxicating.

For the remaining white inhabitants of Trinidad, the island in the 1990s was a strange combination of modern material wealth and 1950s attitudes to women, family and sexuality. It was illegal to be gay then and remains so even today, and divorce was almost as scandalous. Yet despite its galling attitude towards homosexuality, Trinidad is one of the campest places on earth. A curious island, rich with natural resources such as oil, but still suffering the legacy of being tossed between the Spanish, French and then British empires, it is the southernmost island in the Caribbean and feels more South American than its picture-postcard siblings. It has a party culture, not dissimilar in spirit to my own home town of Brighton. If anything remains still for more than eighteen seconds it is at risk of someone reaching for a glue gun and covering it in sequins. Several times a year, it feels as if sequins are the only thing its people are wearing at all, and carnival is the high point of this. It was also the first time I really, sincerely thought about one fact about my body that I had hitherto taken entirely for granted: my whiteness. And the privilege that came with it.

I arrived three weeks before carnival, and I was immediately thrown into a whirlwind of planning with my cousins. Trinidad is a very Catholic island, and its carnival culture originated as a final fling before the deprivations of Lent. Fifty years later, however, the shrinking of the costumes and the event's growing international renown meant that the forty days of abstinence from rich food and drink now more usually took place *before* carnival, and in the name of the body beautiful rather than identifying with Jesus Christ's journey through the wilderness. Even for girls like me and my cousins, raised as fairly strict Catholics, the idea of spending two days dancing around the streets of a capital city in a bikini had created a borderline obsession with diet and exercise, with what seemed like all the women on the island trying to whittle themselves into the best shape possible.

I had only finished my time in the military hospital a few weeks earlier, and stumbled into the midst of this self-denial with an inadvertently slim and toned body. I was comfortable in my carnival costume of bejewelled bikini and headpiece, and enjoyed the party atmosphere. My only self-consciousness was about my Englishness – I felt like a nerd amidst the girls who had grown up on the island, dancing to calypso and confidently parading themselves as the carnival floats set off.

Whatever my inhibitions might have been, the all-encompassing carnival spirit would probably have swept them away. As absurd as the idea of dancing in the street in your sparkly underwear seems, when absolutely everyone around you is doing it too, before long it just feels normal. I was not the sort of teenager who had found her tribe via music. I didn't go to proper gigs, much less festivals, until I was in my twenties and thirties. The exhilaration of feeling music literally pass through your body as vibrations, from the soles of your feet to the roots of your hair, was at this point utterly unfamiliar to me. When we met the parade route on the first morning, the rumble of the huge trucks loaded with speakers turning from a distant bass to an identifiable track, I felt almost sick at the energy which music at that volume could create. Speaking to each other while close to those speakers made our voices quiver. For the first time, I felt music rattle my ribcage and liberate me: it didn't matter if I didn't know the track, let alone the song. I was simply happy to smile, feel the beat of my feet on the tarmac alongside everyone else's, feel the curves of the crowd as we wound our way around the streets of Port of Spain, and feel the bacchanal swallow my words as I whooped and screamed at the sky.

They were two of the most liberating days of my life, in all ways but one: I barely spoke to any people of colour. All of the white people on the island socialised together, had matching costumes and danced together throughout the streets. The lack of integration was staggering to me, as was the absolute silence that surrounded it. And it wasn't just carnival. For the entire trip, it was spelled out again and again. The shopping malls, the members' clubs, the costume fittings. At every turn was this clear visual indication of the balance of power and it was obvious that my lack of melanin meant the advantage was mine.

I felt ill at ease about it at the time, but because no one else was mentioning it, I said nothing. It was as if a spell – benefiting only some islanders – had been cast, and that breaking the silence might mean breaking the spell itself. As if it were something I might break by prising open the silence. For the first time, I was aware of the unearned power my skin colour afforded me. Despite the fun I had there, I never quite shook how uncomfortable the unspoken but obvious segregation of the island made me. But I am ashamed to say that I never acted on it, never researched it, never discussed it. It would be another twenty years before merely knowing a system was prejudiced would turn into knowing what it felt like for your family to be on the receiving end of prejudice.

Within a couple of weeks I was off to spend the rest of the academic year studying and working in Italy. Yes, after spending a month in a bikini, I was heading to a male-dominated world of glamour and idealised femininity. I think we can all wholeheartedly agree that these were hardly feminist bootcamps for a woman on the threshold of adulthood.

*

Britpop was at its height and to be a British girl in Florence was to be cooler than cool, more desirable than I'd ever been. I learned about the attention my body could attract as I strutted through sun-dappled streets to catcalls yelled and kisses blown. I never felt insulted by it, and learned instead to flex that muscle like the biceps I had spent the winter developing. I knew how to change my walk if I wanted attention, I worked out how to get drinks bought for me, I discovered that the quickest way to make more money was to dance dirtier. Before long, I was putting into practice the lessons I had learned in Trinidad. Craving the liberty of small clothes on a lithe body in an atmosphere where you can't hear anyone answer back, I found myself dancing like a bird in a cage on a gilded podium in Meccano nightclub. Leather jackets were blazer style, Chicago house had just hit Italy and the air was laced with the smell of Dolce & Gabbana Pour Homme and fresh wisteria.

At last, my body was not just not bringing me pain, but it was a source of actual pleasure too. Or so I thought. I had no concept of the danger it might put me in until I headed down to the basement of the bar where I worked to get some more *gelato* for the display fridge, only to feel my boss bend over me, the bulge in his black nylon trousers pressing into the back of my thigh as I reached into the chest freezer.

I was young enough to feel that *his* humiliation at being rejected by me would be greater than any risk he posed to my safety. In fact, I interpreted the incident as being entirely my responsibility. After all, I spent all day in my short denim shorts, flirting with customers for tips and having fun behind the bar. Surely a quick grope in the basement was a small price to pay for living a new-found life of such blissful bohemian freedom?

What strikes me most about my diaries at this time is not that I was anxious of being inappropriately touched, of being taken advantage of, or even of being assaulted. Instead I was concerned about my reputation. What would happen if people knew I had behaved inappropriately? I am not sure who my perceived audience – the source of this judgement – might have been. I was slowly – partly through a diet of Madonna albums – becoming aware of the double standards to which Italian women were held in comparison to their men, and with no Catholic family around to make sure I was still going to church, the idea that I must not displease 'the Lord' started to fray. But as an eighteen-year-old I still seemed to cling to the notion that there was some sort of jury out there who could do me damage if they found my behaviour displeasing. Was it my peers I worried about? Was it society at large? I am not sure I really had any grasp on either as independent concepts.

So I spent my time in Italy swinging from rebellious performative 'sexiness' to low-level panic that I wasn't quite pulling it off, or that it might somehow get me into trouble. What I don't remember ever happening during my time there was talking about art, or sculpture, or literature with anyone. I wrote pages and pages about them in my diary, in between obsessive rhapsodies about boys I fancied, friendships I had forged and plans I was making. I was reading late into the night after I finished my shifts, having found an English bookshop which sold everything from E. M. Forster to Hanif Kureishi via Agatha Christie. I would buy copies of *The Face* from the little wagon of foreign newspapers parked in the piazza outside the bar where I worked, its wooden frame dotted with postcards and stamps, then I would read them cover to cover, lying with my legs out on the arch supports of the Ponte Santa Trinita. But my interactions with men were all about my body, which in turn I was quickly learning was all about how other people felt about it.

By the time I started university, I had stopped exercising entirely.

Last year, when I read my diaries from my time spent in the military hospital, I was agog at the detail I had lavished on what, as a life stage, I had so quickly forgotten. I had clearly relished the experience at the time. In those diaries I use the word 'power' more and more with every page, and seem proud of myself in a new way. But if I had not written those teen diaries, and found them in the garage at my parents' house while truffling through my past in the hope of finding clues about the future I was slowly repaving, it would have been as if I had dreamed the entire experience.

How had I forgotten that the entire thing had happened, to the extent that when I took up running fifteen years later, I managed to write a whole book about my exercise journey as a newcomer? Those awakenings I had as I trained for my first marathon seemed absolutely fresh to me, as if I had never felt strength in my thighs or power in my lungs. Was it that I made no lifelong friends there? Was it that the hospital itself closed down only a few years later? Was it that Trinidad, Italy and then university followed in such rapid succession? Or was it that in each of those three new situations, my physical and mental selves once again became entirely separate?

Six months after my arrival at university, the pain was creeping back. I tried to work out from time to time; but with no sense of structure or community, I let it slide. In the hospital, I had felt I belonged, I had been given instructions and told to follow orders, which I had willingly done. But the university gym in mid-nineties Bristol was a very different proposition, filled as it was with rowers, rugby players and the sort of swishy-haired sporty girl I had spent my school years in awe of.

Plus, exercise seemed like a waste of time when there was cider to be drunk and cigarettes to be smoked. The sports guys were boring. Alcohol turned out to be a pretty effective anaesthetic against joint pain when I was dancing. The most I ever did was to sit with my flatmate, transfixed by the Cindy Crawford workout video we had bought. We slumped on the sofa of our shared flat, in black Lycra dresses from the night before, eating crisps and discussing how lovely it must be to have that strength and flexibility. A year before I had had it in spades, but now exercise was a world away, just as my body was once again untethering itself from my sense of self as I neglected to look after it as well as I so recently had. It was easier to accept my flawed body than to try and nurture it. And it let me fit in with the smokers, the drinkers and the partiers, despite my not being sure that that life would let me be my happiest, most effective self. But back then, lacking the role models or the language to reach for anything more, it represented the path of least resistance. So for the next twelve years that is exactly what I did. Nothing.

Things continued this way until my running escapades began, a few months after I turned thirty. Rediscovering what my body could do for me beyond its now fleshier physical attributes was the greatest romance of my life. Exercise was not a closed club for those who already had bodies fit to grace magazine covers, after all! At last, I understood that running was so much more than exercise. It was, it turned out, a powerful tool for boosting my self-esteem, a sanctuary for a head buzzing with anxieties and a way of engaging with the outside world. Learning to run, learning to tether body and mind at last, and then being saved again by swimming, helped me to slip away from old physical assumptions about myself. I was a snake leaving a dried husk behind it, slithering forwards in a glistening new skin. *Running Like a Girl* changed my life in so many ways, but finally being truthful about how I had felt about my body was the biggest change of all.

8

The consequences of being honest about my relationship with my body were unexpected. Within a few weeks of *Running Like a Girl* being published, I was inundated with emails, letters and direct messages all saying variations on the same thing: '*OMG. I thought it was just me.*'

What had initially felt like a leap of faith – admitting the darker thoughts I'd had about my own body and my reluctance to exercise – now felt like a huge consolation. As I had hoped and suspected, I wasn't the only woman who wanted the tools to love her body for more than its shape or size. Nor was I the only one who had felt held back from reaching this point of peace, if not love, by the images which constantly bombarded me of what exercise should look like.

Writing the book and its publication also coincided with the blossoming of my romance with D. Our early days had a constant golden thread of liberation running through them as I talked passionately but with genuine confidence about how I wanted to expand people's perceptions of womanhood. It was the summer of 2012, when the BBC played us endless hours of women competing in the London Olympics: strong, muscly and sweating. Ambitious, ferocious and heroic. Young girls and boys had their minds changed about how many ways there were to be a woman, as I wrote page after page about how we needed to stop apologising for our grit, our dishevelled determination and the very ambition that had once seen us banned from so many sports, lest we become manly. And as I did this, for the first time I had a partner who gave me passionate support and encouragement in this battle against tedious and outdated stereotypes.

But while my inbox and my beloved were telling me one thing, the world outside, specifically the media, was telling me an entirely different story. I had worked in publishing for many years before writing my own books, and I knew that a key part of getting as big an audience as possible to read my work was doing as much publicity as my publishers were able to get. This was a couple of years before Instagram and YouTube 'influencers' had taken off, and glossy magazines and the weekend supplements of the newspapers were the main outlets.

I was lucky: lots of publications wanted me to either write or be interviewed about the revelations running had provided me with. But without exception they wanted an accompanying image. Those commissioning the text usually took a back seat at this point, and my email address would be handed to the picture desk – whose methods I had far less experience of. I would be cc-ed into emails with photographers and assistants, and the words tossed around were all on a theme: 'Fresh!', 'Powerful!', 'Aspirational!', 'Empowering!' Almost always, the request would involve a shoot on the promenade in front of Brighton's admittedly photogenic seafront beach huts. Their candy colours, facing the twin backdrop of the sky and the sea, were an iconic spot in the city.

Usually, these picture desks had not read the book; the decision to use me had been made by the editorial department. So none of them ever took into account the fact that the book was about trying *not* to care what you looked like when running, about unshackling yourself from those pressures for an hour or so a day. *Let yourself sweat,* I was saying. *You'll love yourself far more if you do it and look like crap than if you stay at home looking immaculate.* I joked in the book – and the very features these images would illustrate! – that years of seeing running-magazine and sportswear marketing images of women who looked like the last thing they needed was a good run had left me slumped on the sofa, sure that exercise was a club that I and my wobbliness were not invited to join.

Yes, I had included information on eyelashes and nail polish as colourful and cheering devices that might help me feel less grotty at the mile-twenty slump of a marathon, but in essence I was trying to persuade women to shift the gaze from what they looked like to what they could see if they just got outside and ran for their lives. I wanted to share what it felt like to live within my skin, before and then after running, and how that alteration in perspective had seen my world expand and my life change for the better.

Time after time I was confronted by a team (on the whole, lovely people, keen to do a good job) who had been commissioned to take 'inspirational' photographs of me, and were determined to achieve that goal regardless of what I looked like and what I was capable of. The message was clear: we would really rather you be exactly the sort of blonde, ponytailed, robo-runner who you describe as having intimidated you out of taking part in any exercise for most of your twenties.

Part of the heavy sag in my heart each time I collaborated in these images was the nagging suspicion that I was somehow letting down or misrepresenting myself to my readers. I simply was not giving them the welcome to running that I wanted. A second part of it was that having those photographs taken was so bloody wretched.

On one particularly grim, but not entirely atypical occasion, I was asked – honoured! – to write for one of the Sunday supplements. The inevitable emails about the possibility of shooting on the seafront arrived and, as ever, I tried to point out that the quickly changing light and unpredictable winds on the shoreline usually made it a frustrating environment for photographers. This warning was quickly waved aside.

'What size are you?' asked the male picture editor. 'We'll get something great sent down for you to wear.'

'It's hard to say, as every brand sizes things differently . . .' I tentatively explained. (*A woman would know this is the case,* especially *with sportswear!* I silently seethed.) I tried to clarify that the dimensions of my hips and backside meant I wore larger leggings but that I have short legs so full-length leggings left lots of ruching. I tried to explain that low-cut running tops wouldn't work because of my boobs and narrow shoulders. I received no reply.

On the morning of the shoot, a photographer and make-up artist arrived with a suitcase of designer running gear. It contained items I had silently coveted while doing late-night fantasy online shopping, and almost all of it was in no way going to fit me. As ever, a designer size 'M' is a very different beast from a high-street 'M'. While the imperious Italian make-up artist gave a heavy sigh (at the size of the task which lay ahead?) and laid out all of his kit on the table in my living room, the photographer headed to the seafront to look for spots for the shoot. Meanwhile I went into the room next door and tried to squeeze myself into a variety of garments that were without exception significantly too small for me.

I longed for a girlfriend to giggle at my predicament with: I looked laughable, but felt vulnerable. Leggings designed for supermodels doing the Notting Hill school run pooled around my ankles, creating the impression that I was wearing shiny leg warmers. Some of the glamorous tops didn't even fit over my shoulders, leaving me flapping my forearms like a T-Rex as I tried to wriggle out of them. The garments were made of super hi-tech fabrics interspersed with mysterious twisting seams and mesh segments, leaving sections of my thighs, chest and arms bulging with soft, fleshy urgency.

After a sweaty twenty minutes, I re-emerged and announced to the make-up artist that I would be wearing the thin rainproof jacket that I had found at the bottom of the bag, over leggings which I would yank up beneath it. There were concerns about this combination 'ruining' the line, but I was unmovable. Little did they know how spoiled the lines were yet to be.

My 'natural' make-up was applied for a good forty-five minutes, and my hair tied into a neat ponytail and hairsprayed into submission. Finally, we stepped outside onto the seafront. As predicted, one of Brighton's customary 20mph winds was whistling up and down the beach, rattling the innocent-looking beach huts.

'Let's start off with some running shots,' the photographer gamely suggested, 'and then we can move on to some close-ups.'

He asked me to start by running diagonally past him a few times. After each mini-sprint I stood with a hopeful smile, as he cupped his hands and looked into the digital screen on his camera to check what he had captured. There was no comment beyond a frown.

'Let's try again, except this time, don't *actually* run, just make it look as if you're running.'

'I'm . . . not sure what you mean . . .'

'Well, when your foot is landing, it makes your leg look very heavy.'

'My leg is quite heavy.'

'Yes, but look.' He gestured for me to come and peer at the small screen on the back of his camera. 'Your leg goes like this.'

He pointed. The photographs showed that on account of me not having a mere 2 per cent body fat, when my foot hit the tarmac, my thigh wobbled correspondingly. Sure, it didn't look great. But it did look like a leg in motion. I was at a loss as to how to run differently.

'Maybe try running slower?' came the suggestion. These attempts made my legs no more aesthetically pleasing. I heard a sigh. The make-up artist approached and started spraying my hair back into place. The wind continued to howl.

'What we need is to try and get you with both feet off the ground at the same time. Nice and stretched out. Really empowering-looking.'

'O-*K*.'

'Perhaps we could try with you not running but just doing some jumps. Yes! Just jump from standing and part your legs to look as if you're mid-run.'

'Like Penelope Pitstop?'

'I guess so.'

I stood still, and tried a series of split-leg jumps. I could tell that my feet and the height from the ground was perfect this time. Even my ponytail swished obligingly. But of course because I wasn't running, there was no sense of forward motion in the images, and my boobs had just shot straight up, reaching for my chin. A further sigh.

I felt deeply unpalatable.

Because *Running Like a Girl* was due for publication that spring, these images were being taken a couple of months in advance: in midwinter. I was wearing a vest top and a sheer running jacket, suitable for spring running conditions and time spent in motion. Instead, I was standing in a gale, doing bursts of movement, as icy blasts billowed in and out of my jacket. The make-up artist, snug in a navy puffer jacket and huge boots, shivered and shoved his arms deep into his pockets. He stomped his feet repeatedly. Apparently he was chilly too.

I was asked to sprint (made me too sweaty), to run in the other direction (too much hair blowing into my face) and to stand motionless (eyes watered too much as I stared directly into the wind). The make-up artist became increasingly frustrated at having to pat and gloss my lips to hide the fact that they were tinged with blue, and the photographer remained frustrated that I could not make myself run aspirationally.

I attempted to cheer them up with helpful suggestions that it didn't matter if I didn't look picture perfect, if I wasn't their dream mid-air runner. *The book is about freeing oneself from that!* I tried to persuade them. But brows remained furrowed.

Eventually, after two hours which took me a further four to warm up from, the photograph chosen was one of me crouching, as if at rest after a run, which I like to think my expression implies was hugely aspirational.

This shoot, with its triple hit of male make-up artist, male photographer and arctic headwinds, was the worst of them. But it was by no means an exception: as interest in the book continued to grow, the number I was expected to do rose. With each one, as I eased myself into the bath after wiping the professionally applied foundation away, I felt a little further from the runner I had so proudly described being in the book itself.

It had been those slim-bodied, perky-ponytailed, ever-confident runners who had kept me away from exercise for so long; those images of effortless aerodynamic running which so countered my own juddery plodding and had made me feel my body was not to be enjoyed unless it looked good. And now here I was, complicit in making more of those images, potentially adding to the very problem I had written the book to overcome.

Perhaps I should have been more relaxed about the entire enterprise. After all, these were images to accompany my words – I was not rendered silent in the process, as a model on a sportswear billboard or cover of a runner's magazine was. I was thrilled that people were interested in the book, and was committed to doing the absolute best by my publishers in our joint effort to get as many people as possible to read it. They were just pictures of me having a jog in my home town, after all.

But each piece of publicity was dependent on me committing to having an image taken, rendering me an accomplice in propagating the idea that it wasn't *really* true that it didn't matter what you looked like when you ran. What I was actually helping to spread was the message that it didn't matter what you looked like when you ran . . . as long as you looked like me, with my spray-fixed ponytail, my borrowed designer running kit and who knows what digital alterations that I was not party to.

I was never a true collaborator in these photographs. Nobody ever asked how I wanted to pose, or what impression I wanted to give. In very few of them was I allowed to give any more than a small, enigmatic smile. I was never given any say in which of the images taken on the day were eventually used, and some photographers even declined to show me the full shoot when I asked them. Where my words were at least a conversation between myself and my readers, these images were taking my body and turning it into an obstruction between us. At first I didn't realise this was happening; I gritted my teeth and tried to be a trouper about it. Why complain about cold toes when a well-known magazine wants to lend you its platform to reach further readers? Why act the diva when so many other jobs offer greater discomfort than having to run around a little in the cold? Why be churlish about people wanting you to look your best?

Because it wasn't *my* best. It was *their* best. Those images may have been their perceived ideal me, but they were not me when *I* felt my best. They were me squeezing myself into the very physical ideal that I had railed against and found so much solace in writing about. The images of me at my own best would have been me drenched in sweat after a grim Monday evening run that I had spent two hours trying to avoid but which had changed my mindset for the rest of the week. Or me, arse jiggling and face puce, as I finally realised I had the power to get up a hill that I had only managed to walk up for the first three months of my marathon-training plan. Or me, prone on the sofa, all my double chins out, enjoying a Sunday-night drama with an empty pasta bowl to my left as I felt my blood chug through my system that little bit faster after my longest training run yet. There seemed no way to persuade anyone to use those images. And yet . . . if I had been paying attention I could have been using them myself. Because just around the corner was the Age of Instagram.

My first image was posted on Instagram in spring 2012. It was a heavily filtered shot of some mackerel I spotted at a fish stall on the seafront. I promptly forgot the password for my account and failed to post anything else for months. While others instantly understood its potential both for connecting with strangers and creating a platform which was easy to monetise, I bristled against its focus on mere appearances and stayed hunkered away.

It wasn't until the end of 2014, long after I had married D, that I finally opened a public account in order to reach the readers of *Running Like a Girl* who would still get in touch with me daily.

But trying to engage with Instagram on my own terms this late in the game was akin to hurling myself into a fast-moving river and hoping to wade upstream without getting my hair wet. Four short years after launching, and only two since being bought by Facebook, Instagram had given birth to a visual aesthetic and a financial structure unlike anything I had ever seen or imagined.

With its focus on self-portraiture, it provided a perfect honeypot for those with something to say on how to look, and when I lifted its lid I found it buzzing with clean eaters and 'fitspo' trainers who had swarmed to its sticky edges, creating a hum of advice it was already difficult to look or hear beyond. No one wanted to see what I saw, they only wanted to know what I looked like while doing it.

'Look at what I snapped on my run!' I would say, presenting my profoundly average photograph of a chip being eaten by a seagull. I waited for applause, as proud as a toddler producing a fluff-covered twig from their pocket after a walk in the woods. How sketchily I understood that while I had been busy elsewhere, others had been learning how to balance a phone on an exercise bench in order to capture the perfect angle of their daily squats. Or finding where the best light in their house for photography was, even if it did mean removing a beloved painting in order to create a blank space for selfies. While others still were buying a tripod to discover the perfect angle for a full-length outfit shot. An entire generation had grasped that looking good and promising to share the secret of how to achieve it was a golden ticket to fame and fortune, and all while I had been looking the other way.

How noble I sound, with my lofty ambitions to merely chart the ebb and flow of my local seascapes while others got their hands calloused with the rougher work of holding an iPhone at arm's length and smiling into the good light. Of course I wanted to look great too, it was just that I didn't think I had anything particularly delectable to add. The images flooding the platform had already acquired a specific look: for the most part, that very same ponytailed sporty girl I had spent the last few years railing against, only amplified. Daring to put my own image up alongside them seemed to be asking for judgement: I was going to look like either an unpolished wannabe or a betrayer of my own work. So I stuck doggedly to images of what I saw, what I ate, or what I read, and kept myself out of sight.

But even if I wasn't posting images of myself, I was still following others, and this meant that the suffocating ivy-creep of constant self-reflection still managed to reach me. By now I understood what the platform was doing. I knew that its algorithms preferred faces, that regular posting meant more followers, that there were certain hashtags, tropes or poses that were catnip to users. I saw that people were building virtual empires from these tiny squares. And while I was excited by the idea that women might be making vast, previously untapped amounts of wealth from their bedrooms, entirely circumnavigating the traditional gatekeepers of old media and advertising, I still suspected that it was a world of image over thoughtful content, where a scant few were doing anything genuinely different or lasting. And that ultimately, however sweet the pay cheques seemed to be now, this wasn't women really seizing back control, because the control still lay in the algorithms being written on the other side of the world, by a Silicon Valley man-child who had created the entire empire from a system to . . . rate women's looks.

But having total clarity about this did nothing to stop the lightning-quick mental gymnastics I tumbled through at almost every image I saw. The blur of a somersault as my mind leaped from 'Do I look younger than her?' via an aerobic twist of 'Why *should* I look younger than her, I don't think I actually am?' on to 'Why do I care?' before a final triple spin landing at 'Should I post about all these thoughts instead? Would that be the truly authentic and groundbreaking thing to do?'

Why didn't I just give up on the app, asked those who were not interested in it, or heard me complaining about it? Why bother trying to find a way to make it work when you could just delete it? Because, I argued (and still believe), even if I don't use it, I'm still living in a world partly determined by it. Instagram was now where I found out about books I wanted to read, saw swimming spots I daydreamed of visiting, kept up with friends I no longer lived near, and laughed with family members at photographs of new babies and old memories. Better to stay and be a positive part of it, than to turn my back and know I wasn't involved in trying to make it a less toxic place.

And then there was the fact that it was so extraordinarily compelling. Some days I felt as if I were watching popular culture morph and shift reflecting our collective obsessions and ambitions in real time as those servers on the other side of the world learned more about each of us with every click. My thumbs would be automatically scrolling before I had made the decision to do so, and while part of me was thrilled at this chance to wrestle back some of the control I had so unwillingly surrendered to photographers and magazine picture desks in the past, I was also painfully aware that the power had not truly transferred to me.

There had seemed to be so many ways to be a woman when I was writing *Running Like a Girl*, unpeeling the heroic stories of women who dared to run when forbidden, wallowing in the many different shapes and sizes that runners of all abilities came in, and finding new depths and grit in myself. What had once seemed an inaccessible world had turned out to be welcoming, worthwhile and even life-changing. And now an app full of amateur pictures had captured our collective imagination and seemed to be narrowing that wonderful smorgasbord of womanhood to an even slimmer number of stereotypes than the one I had described in the book itself. The fitness industry was besotted by it, the food industry was swaying woozily between the insanity of cronuts, two-foot rainbow cakes and outrageous undrinkable milkshakes full of biscuits and what looked like gruel. And of course the fashion and beauty industry – which had seemed like it might be having to let in a chink of reality or diversity with the advent of the commonplace women of YouTube – was in thrall to it as well.

As I had sloughed off the self-doubt of my twenties and rattled towards the success of *Running Like A Girl*, I had thought my journey of self-acceptance was happily complete. What adorable naivety! Only a few years later I was struggling to conceive, and the realisation slowly dawned on me that the lessons of self-reliance I had taught myself as I had trained for all those marathons could only get me so far. It turned out that a healthy body might not necessarily provide a simple path to motherhood. I did find a path, but it was painful, uncertain and strewn with obstacles. By then, I was writing *Leap In*, my book about swimming. While writing, I held tight to the lessons that the sea taught me as I struggled with learning to swim: that we should expect, and can embrace, the unexpected. But dealing with the unexpected, in the shadow of an all-knowing algorithm, proved doubly exhausting.

I followed a crop of swimwear- and swimming-related accounts, a choice which quickly revealed the even murkier depths of Bikini Instagram to me. Surfwear is particularly besotted by the image of a lean blonde with sun-bleached hair, but even swimwear brands worn by sensible women doing unglamorous lengths in their local pool or lido were marketed with the male gaze in mind. There was no mention of how you might feel or what wonders you might achieve in swimwear, the implication was as consistent as the running sales-speak of a few years before: don't panic, we can help you look sexy while you sweat. Oh, and if we can't do that we can at least hide the worst of your flaws.

This bitter unfairness reached me like a thumb at the centre of a bruise. Swimming was one of very few things keeping any sense of self-respect alive in me while I endured the emotional and physical punishment of IVF. I was wallowing in despair as I tried and repeatedly failed to get my apparently unwilling body to hold on to one of the number of embryos D and I had made during our gruelling rounds of IVF. Not only was my shape changing as a result of the drugs I was being prescribed, I was also falling out of love with what it could do as it let me down time and again. Now, instead of being sold swimming as the exquisite escape from a mind febrile with anxiety and sorrow, I was being reminded that the biggest problem was how wide my hips might look en route to the shore. Instagram was right there, reinforcing every insecurity. Where the men were sold swimming as a way to get lean, to boost aerobic fitness, to reach out to their inner wildness, their outdoor selves, women were time and again reassured about how to look as small, as flat, as unobtrusive as possible. Here, see if you can slither unnoticed into the water, the ads seemed to be saying. One designer brand's celebrity founder even recommended sitting in the shade, hidden, if you felt you looked too big in your swimwear.

A hopelessness oozed from the phone in my hand straight to my already weary soul as these images reached me, interspersed as they were with my research into the women who had literally drowned one hundred years earlier as a result of being forced to swim in stiff crinolines lest a Victorian gentleman catch sight of a lady's ankle. How few ways there still seemed to be a woman, and how little space for us to do it in.

Cold-water swimming was my salvation during this period, showing me that our bodies are capable of all sorts of surprises, often just at the very moment we have given up on them. Swimmers of all ages, abilities and states of physical and mental health inspired me as I managed to keep myself moving during a period of seemingly endless heartache, and I needed my Instagram feed to reflect that. To my delight, some digging around on the app finally showed me that there was some kick back – the emerging world of Instagram's Body Positivity community.

With its roots in the late 1960s Fat Liberation movement in the US, Body Positivity had arisen from the mire of Instagram's first wave of perfection and its myriad accounts featuring women charting their weight-loss progress, or attempts to 'lead a clean life' using the app as a form of public accountability and/or self-mythologising.

A number of plus-size models, authors and bloggers had made it their self-proclaimed mission to make women love themselves and their bodies, regardless of their shape or size. Some, such as supermodel Ashley Graham, had an enormous platform – well over ten million Instagram followers. This meant regular magazine features and invitations onto mainstays of popular culture such as TheEllenShow – where she was applauded warmly as she gave articulate and likeable no-nonsense interviews about the lunacy of a US size 8 (UK 12) being labelled 'plus size'. Her argument that the fact that 'size 00' had recently been invented by retailers to keep up with the shrinking dimensions of wealthy modern women, and how much pressure that puts on the rest of us to stay teetering within the new boundaries of acceptability, was a compelling one. Others, such as activist and yoga teacher Jessamyn Stanley, were using the platform to reach an audience of almost half a million with images of her fit and flexible, but also fat, black and queer, body in a variety of unapologetic yoga contortions.

A few clicks, and a world had opened to me. The imagination, the boldness, the grace and the beauty that lay within this rich variety of female body types had me transfixed. I seized control of my feed and made it an inspiring place to be. I unfollowed big brands who were steadfastly refusing to use anyone but size 8 women under the age of thirty to showcase their sportswear. Key bloggers and industry names who I felt I 'should be keeping abreast of' went the same way. With that, they ceased to inhabit any further mental real estate in my already crowded emotional landscape. The relief of seeing different shapes, colours and sizes was immense, and I can't have been alone: within the year publications such as *Women's Running* in the UK used a plus-size model on their cover, and brands such as Nike launched ranges with far wider size options than ever before.

So I stayed on Instagram, doggedly trying to inspire readers with images from my swims rather than images of me swimming. Early in my pregnancy, when my publishers talked about organising publicity shots for *Leap In*, I told them I would arrange my own, and did so by paying a photographer friend of mine who knew that I was eight weeks pregnant. He took images of me that we came up with together, after sending each other a variety of images we each admired, and then shot in a secluded environment. Instead of waiting for the arrival of an anonymous photographer with dread, I crept out into the Oxfordshire dawn to a small lake, hunting the best light, wearing no make-up. Instead of hoping to hide curves, I secretly hoped I would be able to spot the first sight of a bump so long yearned for. Empowerment, it turned out, lay in having the money to invest in collaborative images that I felt truly represented me.

By the time my pregnancy was over I was bigger than I had ever been. When I stood on the scales the day before my scheduled Caesarean section, my weight as recorded for the anaesthetist was 100 kilos, and even once I had given birth I felt as if it had barely dipped. Months after the birth, as I struggled to regain strength after my bout of shingles, I was still wearing size 16–18 clothing. In the world of plus-size blogging, campaigning – and living! – this is not that large, and is still at a point in the size spectrum where high-street stores readily stock basics. But for me it felt a world away from the size and dexterity I had enjoyed even when I wasn't at the peak of my running prowess. It was hard to forget that the time I had been at my fittest, I had also been at my happiest, glowing with health and proud of my achievements. Taking good care of myself had been a revelation, a pleasure, a feminist act rather than the deprivation and purgatory I had so long believed 'healthy' living might be. It was also the summer that I had fallen in love for what I sincerely believed would be the last time.

Now, that summer felt far longer than five years ago. As I stood in front of the mirror grimy with loneliness after a series of destabilising experiences, and living in a body which felt not just uncomfortable but alien and profoundly unloved, I needed that body-positivity community more than ever. D seemed to be growing in confidence with every one of L's feeds, while I was scrabbling for a sense of the me I had spent decades building and then learning to love and cherish. But when I turned back to Instagram, it seemed that it had begun to fade and buckle under the white heat of its audience's attention.

By now it was old hat to serve an arresting image of larger women which mainstream media might never have used, accompanied by some thoughtful text. It was clear that word had got out that there was money to be made in the message of body positivity, and suddenly bodies I would love to have been the proud inhabitant of were squeezing their thighs, lifting their 'saggy' boobs and squashing their hands around their stomachs to make as much of a 'flabby belly' as possible. These chunks of flesh were presented to the camera with a beseeching gaze, their owners apparently appealing to the gods of the algorithm. Increasingly, it was commerce disguised as campaigning.

These days, it seemed, it wasn't enough to simply not have the dimensions of a Sweaty Betty model and go about your business. To exist in a digitally unaltered state was to exist in the realms of the *authentic*, perceived authenticity being the algorithm's latest passion – which of course was rendering said authenticity more fragile by the day. The fragility of women's self-esteem had always been jet fuel to Instagram, and now its engines were using greater than ever quantities of that fuel. It no longer made enough of a statement to say, 'This is me, accept it.' By now, stories of self-disgust were getting better numbers than honesty about a sense of unease.

This flesh parade was just a more succulent version of the Instagram I recognised from five years earlier. Women were once again tilting their hips and dipping their chests to the glint of the flashlight just as if it were still 1979.

Sure, it is a gift to see women's bodies of all shapes, spilling out everywhere where once it was only perfect abs and eyebrows to whom the invitation was extended. But the rush to expose in order to 'capitalise on our natural beauty' was essentially devaluing it. Shouldn't we have been asking for payment for our skills, our graft, our expertise, rather than just demanding it for not being afraid to exist as we are? Of course, I understand the urge to share the isolation that comes from seeing relentless female archetypes swarming at you, preventing you from pursuing your passions whether they be running, swimming or simply walking from the bathroom to the bedroom with the lights on when your boyfriend is staying over. And of course I understand the seductiveness of communities based on 'celebrating' diverse bodies, particularly when you've lived uncomfortably for so long in your own.

But this was something else. Or, as Jia Tolentino puts it in *Trick Mirror*, 'Selfhood has become capitalism's last natural resource.' Influencers were by now a legitimate professional field, and their endlessly *authentic* self-presentation was selling everything from T-shirts to cleaning products to yoga mats, via cosmetics, sportswear and injectables. Even body positivity had become a product in itself, and festivals and retreats teaching us how to love ourselves no matter what, started to proliferate.

Now that big-brand companies were involved, the high-spirited online freedom that I had imagined could release me from the rigours of a magazine's picture desk had been replaced by the efforts of an ad agency's Director of Partnerships. And I'm not sure that they were all women. Who was now deciding what was a body worth celebrating? Who was deciding what was diverse versus simply unsellable? What were the new parameters of acceptability, and how were they being measured and policed?

Was this body positivity, or was it in fact a fresh approach to keeping the male gaze firmly on our flanks and folds, waiting for us to – in some cases literally – shake our arses until the purse strings were opened for us? Because it looked like the latter when I searched online anew after a pause for early motherhood.

Despite my discomfort at inhabiting a now so much larger body, the twin horrors of my Harmony test and train assault experiences had done a good job of demonstrating to me that how I looked could offer little protection against medical crises or the larger institutions of the justice system. The assault, in particular, had sharpened my focus as to what impulse lay behind a male reach. It was power, rather than an inability to resist the force of a woman's allure. And I wanted my power back. I wanted to be able to move freely, to wear the clothes I owned, to feel the granite push of my own strength when I lifted my baby. I didn't want the pale compromise of being invited to write a two-hundred-word caption about my muffin top in the hope that someone would send me free moisturiser. And I didn't want to call that positivity.

This corporate gaze on our bodies – making millions for anonymous conglomerates with every click we made – was keeping us ever-looped into a conversation about our looks when we could have been reading, running, drinking, chatting, fucking or just having a quiet cup of tea while the baby slept and telling not a soul about it.

I had hoped that the world of body positivity could give me a boost as I scrabbled to find a fresh way of inhabiting a body I felt increasingly alien from. All of those hours spent with my legs aloft not for a lover or a husband, but for the parade of anonymous experts, passing midwives and anaesthetists whose faces I'll never remember as they led me along the path to motherhood. That magistrate sitting on his raised seat literally looking down on me as he described my pregnant state as too emotional to be a truly reliable witness of my own experience. The drunken hand: the grab made to teach me a lesson. Each had in its own way required me to take a step further away from my own flesh and blood and how I really felt about it.

Now, as I scanned this world of so-called positivity, my overwhelming thought was, *Do I* have *to start loving my body now, no matter what?*

Could I not just head towards feeling neutral about my body, working in companionable silence alongside it? Why must my relationship with it be travelling in only one direction, constantly heading towards more love, more 'fancying myself', more 'feeling my lewk?', more . . . more . . . more? Our bodies change, ebbing and flowing as our hormones trickle through them, our babies fight their way out of them, and our runs, our swims and even our fucks leave their mark on us over the course of a lifetime. And our feelings about how they look and how they serve us shift and shimmy beneath the surface, some left like flotsam on the shore while other worries are worn away until they are grains of sand.

But now body positivity wanted something more of me. It seemed to want *me* to serve *it* rather than the other way around. Was I was expected to keep feeling better and better about my physical self until I died, a self-adoring ninety-year-old in short shorts, a thousand filtered flecks of light dancing around my carefully maintained grey-but-not-quite-natural-grey hair? I was no stranger to the impulse to spend twenty minutes choosing the very best photograph of my swimsuit-clad self before presenting it as an off-the-cuff snap, but now I felt as if I had to share every drop of this maelstrom I was battling rather than concentrating on swimming through it.

When I turned my focus towards the media around new motherhood, I felt that even less of myself, or who I wanted to be, was reflected back at me. Here, nothing was taboo.

Pelvic-floor instability, mental-health concerns, shedding hair, cracked nipples and droopy boobs: so much of this is so important to share. This is particularly true for a generation not always able to be physically close to extended family, constantly being asked to rely on the ever-present internet for solidarity, company and my old frenemy, empowerment. But so much of it had been reduced to a performative exercise in which a community of – largely but not exclusively – straight, white, female, middle-class insta-celebrities had learned how to turn sharing into optimising marketable content. '*Just a bit of reality for ya!*' their captions would say, as if I believed that this image was anything other than as fretted over as my own.

Worst of all was the attendant merchandise. I had longed to be a parent, but I had never yearned for the label MOTHER. I didn't want to be a MUM BOSS. I wanted no part of a club for STRONG GIRLS. Every time the algorithms presented me with a new example of parenting merchandise to achieve the apparently covetable status of Bossing It, Winging It, or Parenting the Shit Out of It, I felt sadder. Sadder that my body's scars and sags were what really branded me a new mother. There was no need for any merchandise. Sadder that there was no longer anyone to bear witness to those changes, and I was still so far from wanting anyone to. Sadder that D, who was proving to be such a loving, imaginative and supportive co-parent, was so far from being a sixty-quid sweatshirt's version of a worthwhile parent. And sadder that there seemed to have been no way out of the bind we found ourselves in, where, decades after feminists first proclaimed our bodies were not our destiny, our bodies still seemed to be our greatest currency.

And if I – an able-bodied, white, middle-class woman – was feeling overwhelmed by this, what must it feel like for all the other bodies out there? What must it feel like for a woman assigned male at birth, who for an entire lifetime has received nothing but daily, hourly, endless messages about what form it is acceptable to live a woman's life in? No wonder, I came to realise, no bloody wonder it might take you nearly forty years to articulate your true self. No wonder you might never say a word, when you already know what society's response will be.

By the time my marriage took its final stumble and eventually fell that autumn, I could see that the path available for women to take was far narrower than it was purporting to be. There were still so many restrictions on how to be an acceptable woman, each of which seemed as prescriptive as anything that had been asked of me in the name of seeming aspirational five years before. But perhaps none were as restrictive as the reality of having been born male.

If I could see nothing like my own situation being reflected back at me, how must it feel to be D? I tried to imagine, spent hours doing my best to empathise. But I could never truly know, because by that point I was on my hands and knees, crawling through the darkness trying to find anything like a course of my own to follow.

9

My first ever Mother's Day lay barely over the threshold of this unfamiliar new life. I spent it with both my mother and my son, me leaning towards her concerned kisses before I dipped to offer L the same on his little squidge-of-burrata cheek. Four months after those autumnal murmurations and the turmoil that had accompanied them, I was starting to feel a little stronger. I had swum through the winter, even as snow had dusted the pebbles of Brighton beach. And I had started to see the first crumbs of a way forward, a space for me to be me again.

Before Christmas, D and I had formalised our decision to separate, although finances and practicalities – I was not yet ready to separate L from living with both parents – meant that D did not move out of our home for a few months. In truth, I was also terrified about being left to look after L on my own. I still felt physically weak, and after being kept in the dark about so much for so long, I was not sure if we would ever see D again once she did move out. So while the three of us slept in separate rooms, we still shared a lot of the night-time disturbances, the bathtimes and the weekends.

It felt like a reprieve, far easier than the sudden departure of a partner on discovering an affair or anything malicious, but it did create a sort of suspended grief for a relationship neither of us wanted to leave but each had accepted was unsustainable. We were utterly united in our love for L and our commitment to navigating this situation in a way that would leave him as unscarred, resilient and brimming with joy as the day he had been born. But as a romantic couple, we were dead.

Christmas had been a frenzied three days of celebration at my sister's house, my extended family radiating love and support, with L glowing as he reflected back at us the love we beamed at him. At once I felt like a discarded Christmas cracker, pulled in two and lost underfoot as the wrapping paper piled up around me – and the luckiest woman in the world. There was not even a second's doubt that L and I would be invited to spend the time together with his cousins. There were no recriminations, no overbearing questions, nothing but a still, clear lake of acceptance. I was at my weakest, but I have never known purer love.

January, as ever, was a different beast. I woke every day to see life through a murky filter of heartbreak. Winter morning after winter morning of opaque skies, while a hamstrung emptiness trickled down the windows with the condensation. Yet, as at Christmas, each morning was also shot through with glorious moments of pure, shimmering love. L, by now a jolly nine-month-old with a soft fuzz of tennis-ball hair, and a smile for everyone from me to the postman or a passing pigeon, made anything seem possible. I would wake up and lean into my pillow to howl as I remembered with horror the reality of my situation, only to be jolted out of my mood just as fast by the appearance of a crawling cherub at my bedroom door, gummily drooling as he made his excited path to my bedside.

Sometimes, while reading, watching TV or simply standing in the kitchen waiting for the ping of the timer, I would look down and see my hand grasping at the air, as if trying to hold on to a past that had slipped out of my reach faster than any ebbing tide I had ever swum in. But just as often, L's delight at something as simple as a slice of apple, a kitchen cupboard filled with plastic storage containers, a leaf falling as his buggy wheeled past, was all-consumingly infectious. He was thrilled by his own toes, enchanted by a washing machine full of old muslins, hysterical at the recycling lorry which drove backwards into our building's car park every Monday morning. It was impossible to see the world as all dark when his outlook was so joyful, so present and so without guile. To see things as he did, daily, was a constant grounding in perspective. Where I had once felt so utterly useless, I now saw how important my role in his life was: I had to protect him from the emotional shrapnel of his parents' explosive past, I had to preserve this sense of joy. I had to find the path.

But night after night as I closed my eyes where once the limbless honey-sweet sleep of early parenthood had found me I would now be set upon by shards of adrenaline. Just as I felt I was ready to rest, my mind finally clear of worries about weaning, returning to work or booking driving lessons, the rage would return.

Sometimes it was thoughts of the choices taken from me that would rattle me like a speeding train, as though someone else was driving my life. For so long, I had believed that the problems we were going through all lay with me. Why was I not breast-feeding properly? Why was I expecting to feel so much happier than I did? Why had I not lost weight faster? Was I too absorbed by the pain that pregnancy and birth had left me in?

The realisation that this missing connection really had never been anything to do with me left me both giddy with freedom and seething with anger. I had not been in possession of the full facts. And the result had been wasted time, wasted energy, wasted . . . me. Oh, the rate at which I could leap from gleeful liberation at knowing I was *blameless*, to fury at how I had been duped. It left me gasping, flailing with a sort of emotional whiplash. If anything, I realised now, those baleful gazes at my post-partum body had been envy towards the very female body I had found such a battleground for so long. They had nothing to do with the repulsion I had long imagined them to.

The grief I felt for the choices I had had snatched from me burrowed deep while the rest of the house slept. I had chosen to marry an unconventional man, but I had not chosen to marry a woman. I had chosen to go through IVF, but because I thought I would be sharing parenthood with my soulmate, not someone who now seemed an utter stranger. I had chosen to try as hard as I did, enduring as much as I had, because I was committed to the long term with someone I thought I knew. How little I had actually known. And so the grief would switch to anger and the night-time cycle would start all over again.

Perhaps, I would ponder on my darker nights, the truth was not that I had tried hard to have a baby with my beloved partner, but that I had been used merely as a vessel for reproduction. I had endured all of that pain, produced the precious baby and then had my reality snatched away. How very convenient that the lie simply could not be kept up any longer – but had managed to hold itself back just long enough for me to try every single one of those embryos, finally, at the very last chance, producing what was needed of me. How very *Handmaid's Tale* it felt on the blackest nights.

I lay seething as the moon rose higher in the sky. I wanted to howl for the invasion I felt my body had undergone. There had never been anything physiologically lacking in me which had required us to have IVF, but it had been *my* body which had taken the brunt of the process. And I had been happy to do it! But oh, how I had misunderstood the terms. It wasn't just the physical burden, the endless needles injected on trains, internal scans taken quickly between meetings, rectal suppositories inserted in bathrooms at parties. It had been an emotional burden too: it had been me who felt the failure at each embryo we lost, despite so little being within my power. It had been me who had been expected to stay calm so each embryo would hold on and stay the course. It had been me who had had to lie just still enough, exercise just gently enough, emote just maternally enough. No doctor had ever found a problem with my body, yet I had just absorbed the narrative that mine would not be 'a real woman's' until it had given birth. It had been impossible to see it any other way.

Now, as I lay in the dark, wondering if the stripe of the moon's light across my sheets would be waking L in the room next door, I felt pillaged. My most powerful years, when I should have been the fittest, the happiest, the most confident, had been stolen from me. Time at the peak of my earning potential, doing work I was genuinely proud of for the first time in my life, had been sidelined. The nature of the treatment meant that I had been the one to hand myself over and I had been the one left physically demolished. It seemed that the invading army, having achieved its aims, had departed, leaving me hollow, weak, alone in the black of night. I was left a husk, while in those grim months it seemed that D, now the parent of a child she would never otherwise have been able to have, was free to start a new life.

I brushed a hand across my sheets as if I could shift the stripe of moonlight lying there. I recalled the time I had seen the author of a book about the moon come off stage at a literary festival. A festival organiser standing at the green-room refreshments table with me asked him about those T-shirts – beloved of eighties and nineties rockers – featuring a wolf howling into the night sky, illuminated by a glowing full moon behind him.

'Why *do* wolves howl at the full moon?' I had asked.

'They howl all month round,' he had replied. 'It's just that we only pay attention when there's moonlight there to illuminate them. Remember, until about a hundred years ago, the only time we could do anything in the dark was at full moon.'

For so long I had been screaming into the night, but now at least I was illuminated by the moon's glow. At long last, here was a situation – our now public separation – which others could understand, a tangible cause for my all-pervasive sadness, a crisis to which people could respond. But it was definitely shadowy moonlight by which we were all working, rather than anything even close to sunlight. What was proving so hard for me, my family and my friendship circle, was the total absence of any sort of script to help us navigate the situation.

Usually, we know our roles. We understand the time for fury, for grief, and for conciliation. We understand what questions are appropriate to ask, which cast members we are permitted to tell vile jokes about, and to whom we apportion blame. We know which songs, which films, which TV shows will console us, either by distraction or by showing a comparable situation (with better lighting) which will see our heartbroken adventurer prevail in the end. We have seen the theatre of break-ups thousands of times before, and we understand what part we have to play in each and every one. Whether it is the naughty friend to go dancing with, the inspiring friend who will text you at 11.59 a.m. on a Sunday to check that you are actually going to get up and get dressed today, or the friend who always knew he was a wrong'un but will never remind you, we understand.

I wanted a map. I wanted someone, somewhere to reflect who I was and what I was trying to achieve. None of the usual tools were available to me. Normal, screaming, blood-curdling rage at a husband who had lied did not – despite my night-time furies – seem to fit. I could too clearly see the wider context in which D's lies had been made for shouting to feel like a viable solution. A celebratory divorce party to *wash the man out of my hair* would feel no better. I didn't want to be single and nor did D, so what was there to celebrate? I had no 'other woman' to heap blame onto, no dashing stranger who had caught my eye. There were feelings, endless feelings, and our culture had utterly failed to provide me with the catharsis I longed for.

*

My family needed somewhere to put their rage as well. My mother, a teacher who has taken trans equality training as part of her job and who has a friend with a trans grandchild, could barely have been more understanding. But her fury at my heartbreak was boundless, and she too felt adrift. Friends were similarly conflicted. They wanted to support me, but felt equally strongly about the vicious hand I had been dealt. And, of course, so many of them were coming to terms with what felt like losing a friend of their own.

Because it did feel like a loss. What I came to realise that spring was that I was not going through a heartbreak but experiencing grief. I know that some trans families resist the idea of 'losing' someone when a loved one transitions – the person is still there, after all. But in my case she still lived with me. Every morning we would be there, treading around our shared child as he crawled at warp speed around the flat, giggling as he went. But it was grief. Not just for the husband I was missing from my future, but grief for five years of memories I was having to recalibrate. What was real? What was I allowed to keep as a treasured memory? And what was just further evidence of how shortsighted I had been?

From time to time I would open my laptop only to be presented with a happy Facebook memory, complete with accompanying image, which left me feeling as if a fist had reached from the screen and punched me in the solar plexus. On one occasion I decided to channel my self-pity into a giant cook-off, experimenting with a new colour chart of pureés to dazzle L with. As I reached to move a cookbook across the shelf, an old shopping list written three years before fell out, and with it what felt like a fat pebble of sorrow from my heart. I recognised my own handwriting immediately, as well as the press release that the list was written on the back of. It was the ingredients for a dish I had made a lot the year we got married, just after my passion for learning to swim had properly taken hold – and with it an endless hunger for swimming. I could remember the shopping trip it had resulted in, and how happy I was.

But was I happy? Now, it seemed as if I was merely deluded, content to blithely brush away signs of either discontent or gender dysphoria in D in a haze of newly-wed bliss. Had I wanted to be loved so badly that I could ignore someone else's pain? On the other hand, how was I supposed to know what these things were? Yes, I had known very little about trans issues when I had met D, but there were also fewer spaces for me to find out about them five years ago. The groundswell of media interest prompted by both *Orange is the New Black* and Caitlyn Jenner's transition had only begun the year that we were married. Before that, unpicking the emotional, political or feminist dynamics of the entire concept had been difficult without knowing where to start, who the reliable voices were, or who were the truly independent journalists. Perhaps my biggest misunderstanding was the idea that the essential 'knowing' that one might be trans and then being able to express it was a simple, linear process, rather than something that one might deny to oneself, sweeping it into corners where it was easier not to look, then stamping it down lest it should ever be said aloud.

I watched anxious documentaries featuring small children expressing themselves with the only vocabulary they understood, clinging to playground notions of pink and blue toys as if they were the only markers of identity, which merely served to create a greater environment of uncertainty. All the while, different ends of the political and libertarian spectrums panicked about these children being either dismissed or 'over-diagnosed'. Who was the voice of reason here? How to unpick the data? How to offer genuine support without exacerbating problems? These questions alongside the swift evolution of terms and acronyms made me feel very far from being able to discuss the issue effectively.

So I didn't. I got on with my life. Which of course left me with this barrage of questions. Who had I even been in love with? A figment of my imagination, or D's? A fantasy husband who was such good company, so supportive, so empathetic . . . because that man was in fact a woman? Were the things that I thought made D such an exceptionally wonderful man, the same things that meant D was actually a woman? These moments, these streams of memory and experience now had to be re-contextualised, creating psychological maelstroms that I would have to pick my way across, exhausting me. The genuine weight upon my heart felt physically painful for months, leaving me drained as I carried on with the day-to-day routines of caring for an infant.

I knew I had not imagined that husband. That shopping list was written in bliss even if not, as it turned out, an untempered bliss. I could remember the jumper D was wearing the day I wrote it. I could remember the warmth of that chest beneath my hand. That love was real, it had had two beating hearts. But the person I had been in love with had vanished. And so I grieved.

A driving lesson which ended up taking us down the road where we had had therapy during IVF treatment; a T-shirt of D's that I wore in bed during pregnancy which resurfaced in a basket of outgrown babygros; a shift in the light as the clocks changed which reminded me of the hope I had been brimming with in the month before L was born, now nearly a year ago. Each of these things provoked waves of grief for a husband who seemed to have slipped away like shingle after a momentous tide.

When I found that shopping list I left the kitchen, baby food spilling from bowls on both countertops, and went into my bedroom. I was almost too weak with sadness to stand. I put my hand up on my bedroom wall to support myself and stared at the dent on my ring finger where my wedding band used to be. It seemed no inch of my body had been left without an imprint of these last few years. I pushed at the wall, willing it to give way, to turn marshmallow and simply absorb my hand, my arm and then all of me.

But other days, as spring slowly crept up on me, I could see my freedom for what it was: a life without lies, a life full of fresh choices, a life in which L would never have to grieve for a father he had made a connection with: he would only ever know the two of us as we were now.

And it was L who showed me the light. I had no role models, and I could see none for L. So we would have to stomp through the undergrowth and make our own path. By spring people were starting to worry that I was sweeping things under the carpet, that I seemed too *OK*, that I was not angry enough for a woman coming out of the sudden break-up of a marriage.

Or were they concerned that I was suffering from insufficient shame for a woman who some thought had been roundly humiliated by her spouse?

The breakdown of your marriage shows strange fault lines in the relationships of those around you. Some couples I knew socially appeared to suspect that divorce was somehow contagious, asking me hurried, whispered questions about signs I had seen, things I wished I had responded to differently, fights I wished I had picked.

You guys seemed so happy and you were hiding this? they seemed to want to say. *What on earth does this mean I could be getting wrong about my own marriage?*

Some were panicked by things that simply did not seem a priority to me. Would L be bullied at school in ten years' time? How would I cope with my lonely weekends when L started to spend half of them with D? How would I find a new partner quickly enough to rebalance their dinner-table requirements? Others, meanwhile, seemed to almost require from me signs of the same level of rage that they would feel. Some seemed braced for more sadness than I felt, some for more despair. Just because I wasn't performing it didn't mean I wasn't feeling it, but nor did I feel that I was obliged to adhere to any script or social norm – especially because there was no real guide for my situation. If I was expected to do the hard grind of finding a path forward without role models or representatives, I wasn't prepared to be restricted to a preordained divorce narrative. Most of all, nor was I prepared to express an anti-trans sentiment that I simply didn't feel – no matter how others might have expected me to respond.

It was becoming more than clear to me that anti-trans sentiment was a huge part of how D and I had got here. Yes, I felt as if huge areas of my identity had been trampled on. Yes, I felt confused by what it meant for my body, my sexuality, my sexiness that my husband was a woman. And yes, I felt furious that we had got so far into a marriage that the course of my life had been permanently changed by parenthood, but with someone I could never stay married to. Whichever way I looked at our predicament one thing was always as clear as day: if D had grown up in a world where she had been able to admit to the feelings she had without fear of losing love, status or even her life, then the confusion that had come my way would simply never have had cause to exist. D was responsible for that confusion, but I never, ever felt that she alone was to blame for it.

While my feelings raged on, D was dealing with a health service which – even in Brighton's LGBT+ bubble – meant a waiting list of three years at best before even being given an appointment at a gender identity clinic, let alone having the appointment itself. Where I had feared she would vanish from our lives in search of new thrills, she was in fact beginning a physical and emotional slog every bit as demanding as mine. She was dealing with discussing transition with family, friends and colleagues. She lost a not inconsiderable number of these people by simply telling the truth. And throughout it all she was still present at bedtimes, overnight babysitting and every key doctor's appointment L has ever had. She has been financially honourable and responsible as a parent. She always was, and has never been less than, a good, loving and decent person. And the very hilarity which was the golden thread sewn through our courtship is now enjoyed almost daily with our son. The true tragedy of our marriage is that if, even decades before we even met, she had felt that she was able to confess the feelings she felt instead of learning to repress them – time and again, with every tawdry sitcom episode, ill thought-out newspaper column or cheap stand-up gag – then huge ripples of people could have been spared so much pain and confusion. If her childhood had had any role models beyond cartoonish tabloid stories about truckers in heels, sleazy MPs or models with jawlines just a little too manly, there might have been a suggestion that she might not just survive but thrive when living her life truly as herself.

I had already known trans people before I realised the reality of D's position. And while my friends were largely sympathetic to the trans movement, I understood only too clearly that the world beyond my Brighton community could be far less so. I was powerfully aware that there would forever be a possibility of prejudice towards D, and that that could in turn go on to impact L's life. And I understood that all the more clearly now because until relatively recently I had sometimes been guilty of not giving it much thought at all. I had never felt anything as strong as 'anti-trans', but I had certainly misunderstood the weight of the pain that the thoughtless use of a pronoun could cause, or underestimated the risk that trans people – particularly women – expose themselves to when they come out (according to the 2018 Stonewall report, in the preceding year 41 per cent of trans people had experienced a hate crime or incident, 28 per cent had faced domestic abuse from a partner and 12 per cent had been physically attacked by colleagues or customers at work. These are not things you expose yourself to on a whim). I now knew how easy it was to be careless with throwaway comments, to be anxious about listening to challenging ideas or even lazy with trying to use unfamiliar terms or phrases.

Until not long before, I had found the performative hyper-femininity that a lot of female-born women can associate with trans women very uncomfortable. The most famous example is of course Caitlyn Jenner. The heels, the hair, the pout – a Hollywood version of a woman. To the woman who is exhausted by being expected to paint on a lipstick smile for her boss every dreary Monday morning, or the woman who longs to wear trainers on a big night out but daren't be the only one a foot shorter than the rest in the group photographs, or the woman who is called 'blokey' for having the short haircut she feels comfortable with, this kind of womanhood can feel like it is undermining everything she longs to escape. It can feel like a further straitjacket buckled with stereotypes, imposed by someone who has slithered chameleon-like on to her team, while having already enjoyed the advantages of the other's. It *can* feel like that: but it doesn't have to.

D, who had always been a fairly androgynous dresser, did not start wearing florals or leopard print overnight. Day-to-day clothing remained largely the same, but I did on occasion watch the introduction of foundation, eyeliner and lipstick, and think, *You did all this so you could wear make-up?*

Now, a few short months later, I saw the situation from the very opposite angle. Had I not learned to perform womanhood myself? From the covers of those same magazines I went on to appear in? On that podium in Italy, along those streets of Trinidad, in those heels newly bought for working in an office? I can remember the swish of my first handbag as clearly as I remember the cool leather strap of the one I was wearing the day I was assaulted. The former bag swung against my hip, entirely empty of anything useful, yet a badge of honour for having made it to womanhood. The latter, filled with things the adult woman longed to leave behind some days, also labelled me as a woman as I stood in court being told it was the handbag which had touched my body, not a hot male hand.

Even as I watched D's slow evolution, I could remember standing in the bathroom of my parents' married quarters on a German military barracks. A glum autumn evening when my younger siblings were downstairs watching *Noel's House Party* and I stood in the bathroom, desperately squeezing flesh from the sides of my ribcage to see what I'd look like with a cleavage. I scooped and I pressed, longing to see what the world was telling me was a woman's figure. I yearned for the process to hurry up, for an external signifier of the changes I felt I was undergoing. Now, though I had never been surer of my status as a woman, I longed to perform the very opposite on my new enormous post-partum bosom.

It seemed like yesterday that I would sit on my parents' double bed, watching my mother apply her daily make-up from over her shoulder. Her perfume, three carefully saved and eked-out glass bottles on the left of her dressing table. Her make-up in the right-hand drawer, her hairbrush and moisturiser in the left. The day-to-day rouge and mascara I would watch her sure hands apply with practised swooshes. And the pots of glitter for special occasions that I knew lay further back in the drawer. Occasionally, if she wasn't too busy, I would be allowed to see the peacock greens and blues, and once or twice even dip my finger in the glittery pool, wiping it across the back of my hand and watching the sparkles dance under the light coming from the window behind me.

I have never felt safer, more welcomed or respected in someone else's private space than I did in those moments. This was where my mother became the person she wanted to present to the world every morning. It was only a few minutes, but it was time she took, unselfconsciously, to brace herself for life as a woman. And I was not just privy to it, but invited: it was a branch-line station on the tracks which would take me to my destination as a woman. I thought of D, never openly welcomed or invited to witness such a delicate ritual, how she had pieced it together from popular culture, imagination and stolen glances. No wonder not every trans woman's chosen appearance in the early days of transition hits the right note for every one of the other women who had always been welcomed to the party. How could it ever?

And I remembered my adolescence and early adult years, when I learned to wield womanhood as a weapon, and would do so whenever I could. It was the golden age of Girl Power. If you had just enough alcopop in you, you could think of something sassy to say back to anyone who demeaned you, harassed you, or groped you. Because you were desirable, and therefore you had won anyway. We were told we could do anything, be anything, if we stayed positive and just the right side of sexy. Above all, being a woman who got ahead was to be a woman who fitted in and looked the part. White, cute and up for anything.

This was learned. I had no instinct for this. I just had long summer holidays with a lot of MTV and a lot of student bars full of men who thought you were an equal if you could drink as many whisky Macs as them and still make it to lectures on time.

So now, when I hear women complain about the performative femininity that trans women sometimes display I wonder, *What were you like at fifteen, eighteen, twenty-one? A sturdy feminist untouched by this culture we've created? A woman born with intrinsic talents for perfect eyebrows and five-minute blow-drys? Did you have to learn too, or were you strong enough from childhood to shun it, come what may?*

The memories of me fighting not to feel like less of a woman because I hadn't found an effortless path to pregnancy were too fresh for me to start judging the required biology for entry into womanhood that D was experiencing. I had taken oestrogen, I had undergone surgeries, I had manipulated nature in order to live the life that I felt would be my very best. How could I now expect a different standard from others?

While I was undergoing IVF treatment I found myself fascinated by the different biological and societal markers that make a woman, how different medical disciplines prioritise different indicators, and how that has shifted over the generations. Melodramatic though it may seem (and perhaps because I was reading *Wolf Hall* at the time) I often thought of Anne Boleyn and each of the three miscarriages she had after giving birth to Elizabeth I, while the nation – and her husband –

longed for a future king. At least not staying pregnant doesn't mean your life is literally in peril, I would tell myself on my glummer days. The sheer horror of waiting month after month, desperate for a biological function you had absolutely no control over, used to haunt me. Oh, Anne.

Generations of women had been deemed less than a woman because they couldn't fulfil certain biological imperatives. For centuries it had only been those with basic externally visible genitalia, or even those who could produce children, who would pass muster. Then, at the turn of the twentieth century, the discovery of the XY chromosome sex-determination system became the definitive test. Then came the ability to test for hormone levels and, with that, further debate about what the normal or appropriate levels might be. As science has developed and our knowledge both of the human body and of human behaviour have grown, what definitively determines what a woman *is* has shifted as much over time as what defines a 'good' one.

A few months into our new family format, I was as sure as I had ever been that there were many – possibly infinite – ways to be a woman, and that they should always include trans women. Yes, I was still stumbling over pronouns and riding out my own waves of rage and grief. But if we are to tell our sisters that they may – and should! – present themselves in whatever way makes them feel comfortable, we cannot then discriminate against those trans women who may have shoulders too broad or jaws too square to make us personally feel comfortable. It made no sense to me when I read women calling themselves 'gender critical feminists' saying that female-born women should be allowed to be as butch as they like without fear of erasure or pressure to transition, but also saying only a breath later that trans women were grotesque parodies of women. Surely we either broaden the definition of womanhood in both directions, or we stay in the dark ages?

It wasn't just D that I wanted to protect. Of course, L was my primary concern. With every day that passed, I understood more and more the need for representation both for trans children and their parents, and for families with trans parents. I longed for not just role models but a reflection of his family for L as he grew up. I also retrospectively longed for them for the lonely child that I now imagined D must have been.

Meanwhile, I was aware that people beyond my wider social circle now knew that my marriage had broken down. People I knew professionally, readers of my work, contacts I had known for years but would not normally share personal information with. In those months, I had become increasingly convinced of the positives of my situation – and the longer I didn't share the truth, the longer I was keeping these positives at arm's length. I worried that people might assume that the pressures of IVF, or even the hard work of early parenthood, had been our undoing. I did not want to let the truth slip away from people. So on L's first birthday, emboldened by the advent of spring and the need to celebrate, I wrote an Instagram post briefly outlining the facts of our new set-up. I chose a photograph of L and me underwater, our eyes locked, our hair splayed, our skin touching. I wrote, I reread. I reread again, understanding that the internet doesn't let you take back a fleeting moment of honesty, and finally, I pressed 'post'.

L's birthday! A whole year of L! I can't believe it. His middle name is Joy and he really is joyful every day. Here is a pic from six months ago at swimming class. Being in the water with him has been one of the greatest happinesses of the last year, which has been, erm, challenging.

I'm very aware that a lot of people come and find me here after reading *Leap In* and want to know how things turned out. For some of you it must be a bit lurch-in-the-stomach to see baby pics if your fertility experiences aren't as positive, so please have a huge hug from me and know that I will never ever ever forget those years of wrestling to convince myself I was still 'a success' if I never had a baby. WE ALL ARE!

And there has been even more wrestling with my emotions these last six months or so, as it turns out L's other parent has made the decision to transition. It's not something I was expecting – by any stretch of the imagination. And it is something that means my little family, while still awash with love, is becoming a very different shape: L is now part of an LGBT+ family, albeit one with two adoring parents who are renegotiating what family can be, and I am heading into the future single.

I'll probably write about all this at some point, as it is a strange spot to be in when trans stories seem to be everywhere but not one is representing your strange, joyful, heartbreaking experience. I'm

> pretty sure it isn't *just* me and, um, Kris Kardashian, but at times that is what it has felt like – which has been a lonely old place to be! So thank you very much, Lovely Instagram People, for being so kind and filled with advice and warmth and positivity this last year or so. I have never wanted for driving advice or wild garlic recipes or weaning tips, or even just people dropping me a line to check if I'm OK, and it has meant the world during a very rocky time. Onwards, with joy! xxx

Then we took L for birthday pizza.

I had expected some polite clicks on that post, and perhaps a few text messages from people who knew my number. What I had not expected was the huge rush of warmth and empathy from so many thousands of people. Where a few days earlier I had worried that a discreet silence had been calcifying into the keeping of yet another harmful secret, I had smashed the rumours by being open, determined never to let fear of living truthfully hold my family back again. The relief was enormous.

10

Laying the brickwork of our new path had begun. And I was determined that the one my family took would now be a wider one. Because I had learned, on a visceral level, how truly lucky I was to be born with everything I had. My body, for all the pain, heartache and disadvantages it had presented me, nevertheless set me at a huge advantage in comparison to so many others. Yes, I longed to be fitter again, but my body was still largely healthy. The colour of my skin did not leave me open to discrimination in my daily life from the workplace to the maternity ward. The body I was born in did not leave me open to hate and prejudice in the way that D's now did, or any of my other LGBT+ friends' did. I had always been sympathetic to those who faced discrimination, but now I had some insight into what it felt like to be 'other'.

I had skin in the game. I had, my mother told me with typical restraint, become radicalised.

And in a way, I had. If the Oxford Dictionary defines 'radical' as someone who 'supports great social or political change', then that is exactly what I had become. I had realised that the only way I could truly be comfortable in my own skin was by being ruthlessly honest, and committing to being an ally of the

LGBT+ community. And not just that community, but any disadvantaged group that was not part of the narrow mainstream.

This was not an act of altruism, but one of survival. This shift from knowing that a situation was unjust, to actually feeling it, was enormous. Where I used to nod and agree – and then do nothing – when I heard discussions about lack of representation in children's books or cartoons, I now experienced them on a physiological level: the quickening of my heartbeat as we entered the library, a playgroup, or even a new friend's house as I checked for signs that L would not be the only infant with a 'different' home set-up. The bags under my eyes were the evidence of sleep lost to hunting for literature and TV that might show L a family like his own – and before he learned to say the word 'family' itself. I shocked myself by bursting into tears when I saw the first photograph of Prince Harry and Meghan Markle holding their new son. Not because of any royalist sentiment, but because I now knew how much it meant to see a family with such status proudly displaying their diversity. I thought back to that unease I had felt in Trinidad and how I had said nothing, how my silence had helped maintain the illusion of safety. Well that illusion was now gone.

I had to be part of changing what a family could look like, and if I was going to do it for LGBT+ families, then I was going to have to do it for all families that varied from the straight, white, able-bodied norm. I had to be part of changing what it is possible to embrace as a modern woman, to help create a world I could bear for L to grow up in. I knew what it felt like to get on the bus slightly behind D as she pushed the buggy, and see the faces, ranging from the curious to the judgemental, turning in her wake. The scornful or, at best, confused faces, wondering how a woman who looks like she does is in charge of an infant. I have been to a museum with her and had to take a different route around the exhibition to protect our family from the sneers of other visitors, L thankfully oblivious all the while.

I knew that this all had to be challenged. To stay silent would render me complicit in the judgement. I knew what it had taken me to go to nursery the week before L started and beg them not to only read him books with 'a mummy and a daddy', because our family had radically changed since we had registered him for a place. I knew what it felt like to hear doctors, shop assistants and mummy bloggers referring to 'the father' when I knew my child would never have one.

For the rest of my life, I will be explaining to those who casually assume they know what shape a family is. Already, I have done it hundreds of times, and soon L will start doing it too: learning to stand tall, look directly at whoever is behind the desk at the GP's, the passport office, the parents' evening or wherever and say, 'This is the shape my family is, and that is OK.' To learn to smile, accept their apologies or ignore their quips and take another step down our path.

To hold my head high, looking life square in the eyes, and say with confidence that while D was no longer my partner the three of us would be for ever family – and that I was proud of what we could achieve together – was the only possible option. And as with every walk, every run, every swim I ever took, it wouldn't be until I got going that my heart would find its rhythm, my legs their pace, and my head its equilibrium.

It wasn't an easy stance to adopt. Yes, there had been decades of frustration at how I might be treated differently on account of being a woman. The sheer tedium of having to wonder if the bike repair shop guy is patronising me because I don't look like a Weekend Wiggins. The scrabble to find my keys in my pocket as I walk home from the station in the dark sensing that a man is walking behind me. The grim feeling of hearing yet another insult yelled as you run past a bench of adolescent boys.

But I also had decades of knowing that I didn't really challenge people when I walked into a room. I sound educated, I can explain myself well, and at a casual glance I look like just another Breton-top-, gold-hoop-, Nike-Air-Max-wearing middle-class mum.

Now I had to learn what to do with my face while strangers decided what to do with theirs on hearing about my set-up. For L's sake I had to learn new terms, research developmental milestones in language development and read up on government consultations about trans rights. And in doing so I found corners of the internet – and mainstream media – where I saw not just prejudice but wilful, unapologetic hate of the sort which had never in a lifetime been directed at me or my family. Dealing with this was akin to trying to use muscles for the very first time. And I had to do it while getting used to living alone with someone who had only just learned to walk.

Some of this was astonishingly hard work. I was trying to resurrect my career with only two days a week of childcare – writing a proposal for, and waiting to hear news on, my first fiction deal. I went back to my regular slot on the radio, I started chairing events again, I had endless meetings in London to remind people that I was back and ready to work. Each time, I had to allow for a moment to 'explain things', before returning in time for nursery pick-up.

It was the endless heatwave summer of 2018, and there was not a single sunny day that I didn't feel grateful for. We made the most of our seaside city in every possible way. We sat on the beach, L and his best friend mushing strawberries into their gummy mouths, as much in curiosity at the texture as ecstasy at the juicy sweetness. We woke early and sat ripping croissants apart in the shade of buttercream Regency squares, and when we had finished our pastries we crawled amidst the flowers checking for bees. We walked everywhere, L face out in his buggy, waving at buses, diggers and even faces he was starting to recognise from nursery.

At night, when he was softly snoring, I wore my worst, ugliest knickers and greyest grubbiest T-shirts while I lay spreadeagled on the living-room carpet, drinking ice-cold white wine as the sun went down and flicking between *Love Island* and the *World Cup*. I had been braced for the lonely emptiness of the flat overwhelming me once D left, but when it actually came I seemed to inhale, a little stronger each time, and fill the space with a new sense of daring, that I might cope after all.

I was too exhausted to worry about dating, too drained at the end of each day to worry about trying to make myself delectable for anyone else. The sweet liberty of basking in those uninterrupted evening hours like a cat on a sun-warmed windowsill gave me hope that I might one day return to a sense of peace with my body. After so many high-shouldered months while I tried to figure out what was wrong with me, I needed that summer to do absolutely nothing at all about my physical self. I just needed to let it be, to let myself exist unexamined, unimportant, un-meddled with.

There was some emotional work to do too. While the end of my marriage had been a huge blow, it wasn't the only one I had suffered. I had to do a sort of emotional audit, working out where the pockets of anger that would still spring up from time to time actually belonged. D could not – and should not – bear the weight of them all. Eventually, I made a series of formal complaints about my experience with the Harmony test, and got in touch with the fertility clinic in West Hove who had so honourably stepped up to help us at the time. Finally, I was able to say a proper thank you – not just for the help but for our son.

The National Midwifery Council came back to me some weeks later saying that I had been treated by the Harmony test practitioner in their capacity as a sonographer, not a midwife, and as that is an unregulated industry it was beyond their remit. I took legal advice, was told what a good case I had, then looked into the golden grin of my son before deciding that enough of our time together had already been wasted on painful admin. I took it no further.

Last year, however, when a friend announced that she was pregnant and that she had been for a private scan outside the city, I felt my body shake as I softly asked where. When she told me, I had to leave the room. I quietly vomited in her bathroom, not wanting to sow in her the seeds of panic that I had endured as a result of that place. When, once her own baby had been born and I could hold him in my arms as L tried insistently to stroke his hair, I told her everything, I felt that at last this episode was over.

These blips and blurts of emotion, these moments in which what I had been through would unexpectedly seep into what was otherwise turning into such a happy time, would often take me aback. It was only with hindsight that I began to understand just how much I was trying to process, and certain things fell by the wayside. My hair, at last growing back after the fistfuls that had fallen out post-shingles, went uncut for over a year. I simply didn't have the mental bandwidth to make a decision about what sort of haircut I might actually *want*, so morning after morning it was scraped back into a ponytail and forgotten about. Random bills would occasionally go entirely unpaid until scary letters arrived, and to my shame I forgot more of my family and friends' birthdays than I had ever done before. It was, I suppose, a sort of cumulative post-traumatic shock. My heart and mind were humming with the effort of what they were ploughing through. Sometimes as I lay there in my grotty T-shirt I felt I was whirring like a laptop with too many tabs open.

I had been taking L to swimming lessons in central Brighton for over a year (since he was only eight weeks old), when I was confused by his sudden anxiety in the classes. None of the other children seemed to be behaving like this, and he had always been so happy there. It felt as if it had been me and him in a tight watery embrace since he was born, while the world splashed around us. The weekly half-hours we spent at that pool were some of our most special times together. The shared adventure, the whoops of achievement, the honey-sweet nap immediately afterwards. Out of nowhere came panic.

It was only our beloved – and perceptive – instructor who unravelled the problem, taking me aside after the third week when unhappy wailing had replaced peals of giggles.

'You've lost your nerve,' she told me. 'It isn't him, it's you.'

She was quite right. Where I had once immersed L without a second thought, just happy to be the sole focus of his attention in those very early months, the older he had become, the more connected we felt. As this bond had been tightened, I had started to pause, a second's panic before I dipped him underwater. Where six months previously I had been dealing with trauma of such immediate and overwhelming magnitude, now those anxieties were loosening their grip, leaving me space to consider, albeit unconsciously, that dunking your baby underwater can be terrifying.

L in turn – not used to this hesitation – was exhaling during that second's pause, leaving him breathless just as I eventually dunked him. No wonder he had started to hate the pool, the unhappy victim of my mental churning. The teacher told us to play at the side of the pool for a couple of weeks which we happily did. Before long, our collective confidence returned, a tiny step which nevertheless felt like a huge one.

There was also the assault and ensuing court case to recover from. The sense of frustration I felt at how it had gone was only mitigated by the kindness I had been shown by the women around me at the time. Even now I have moments of boiling rage at the complacency with which a warm hand was described as so similar to a handbag. To take the law as far as I could and still be told my truth wasn't real. I decided I had to make something constructive come of the anger, to do something to support women rather than just spend fretful hours pondering our relative vulnerability. And I was lucky enough to be presented with an opportunity just when I needed it.

It was around this time that RISE, a local charity helping people who had been affected by domestic abuse, contacted me. I had been in touch with them a few months earlier regarding a donation of some toys that L had grown out of, and we had remained in touch on social media. They asked me whether – as the author of *Running Like a Girl* – I would consider helping them with some of their fundraising. Two of their main charitable functions were running events, so I said yes, I would love to come and talk about how I might get involved.

But I was nervous.

I wanted to support them, of course I did. I was painfully aware that any trauma I had suffered over the last couple of years was nothing in comparison to that suffered by women in violent or emotionally abusive homes. And yet I was also painfully aware that gender-critical feminists continued to insist that trans women should not under any circumstances be allowed into single sex spaces. I had often wondered whether this was a position that women's refuges themselves took. Because while I was prepared to trust that those on the front line of these sorts of services must surely know best, it also sounded grimly unfair.

By this point D and I had done a lot to build a new relationship with one another. Not a romantic one, but one that runs far deeper than friendship and that is as engaged as any other family. We had managed to avoid becoming one of those ex-couples who could not be in the same room together. We had fun indulging L's curiosity, including taking him for mussels and fries.

By now the trust between D and me was coming back as never before. The corrosion of trust, what then felt like furtive behaviour had taken hold of our marriage so quickly and so suddenly that undoing it took time and effort, but D succeeded in surpassing all my expectations. We are not wealthy – we had not yet bought a home – but we have never argued about money. D has been consistent week in, week out, in a way that is rare even in some ongoing marriages. The family ties that we always promised we would try and maintain for L grew around us, a network I never dreamed the three of us would ever have, let alone cherish.

I looked forward to seeing her when she came over – several times a week – for bath and bedtime. I enjoyed our chats once L had fallen asleep. I still do. We continued to text each other just as many silly photos and videos of L at play, asleep in the buggy or up to mischief, as we ever had. The steel frame of the friendship upon which our romance was built remained, revealing itself over time as the rubble of our marriage crumbled around it. D still makes me laugh as much as anyone I have ever known. And more than that, she has re-earned my trust.

So it wasn't just noble agenda-setting or maternal instinct that made me wary as I approached this meeting at RISE. I have seen the abuse that trans women face in day-to-day life, and I didn't want to be a part of perpetuating that. I have supported D when she has arrived at the flat, shaking after having had abuse shouted at her in the street on the walk over. I see the looks, I see them every day. I hear the muttered comments from men who otherwise appear to be enjoying a Saturday out at the seaside with their family. And I see the pain and frustration when birthday cards, texts or work appraisals still arrive with pronouns or titles that reveal so much about how she is still seen by some. I see the vulnerability in her. I see the fear if we have to wait at the bus stop on the same day that the football fans are there, riled up. I know that fear, and I know that she is now one of us. And we are *all* in the same fight – sometimes for our lives – against gender-based violence and the tiresome constructs that state our bodies are what determine our position in society.

So the idea that I might work with a charity that would refuse to welcome D if she found herself in an abusive situation would be intolerable. But there was only one way to find out what sort of an organisation RISE were. It was late spring, the sort of day that could start off freezing cold but feel like the promise of summer if you walked on the sunny side of the street an hour later. I was sweating with nerves and the effort of pushing the buggy up the hill. L was shouting 'TREE!' and then squeaking with little 'OOH!'s as I pressed the coloured buttons for the lift and eventually arrived at their offices. It wasn't just what I had to ask them that was making me nervous, but what it represented: it was the first time that I had had to confront this new reality, to truly stand up and be prepared to act on what I believed in a public capacity. It was the first time that for L's sake, if nothing else, I had to live my life honestly and without shame – even if that meant walking away from something that I wanted to do.

The team members led us into their staffroom and were immediately welcoming and lovely. We made amiable chit-chat while L played with the little pile of toys they had put out for him. I swallowed hard and drank greedily from the glass of water they handed me. Seeing the little dimpled chub of L's fingers on those toys which had been played with by children in so much distress pulled me back to myself.

'First of all, are there any questions you have about us and our work?' asked one of the staff.

'Well, yes, there is one. But I'm ashamed to say it's somewhat about me and my situation . . .' I began.

'Go ahead,' said Jo, the charity's director.

'Well, I'm not sure if you follow me on social media, but perhaps you saw my recent Instagram post on L's birthday last year?'

'No, I don't think any of us use Instagram,' said Jo before looking around the room. The others shook their heads. Oh. Using that post as a shortcut was not going to work. It was time to take a deep breath.

'Well, last year, when L was a bit smaller, I found out that my husband had realised that they were going to transition. They are . . . a trans woman . . .'

The eyes looking back at me were not narrowed with fear or judgement, but soft with empathy.

'. . . and while I have obviously been through a great deal of heartache, I support that decision. D is a great person and a great parent. And I support her, for L's sake as much as mine or D's. And while I appreciate the fears that some people have, I don't feel like I can be aligned with an organisation which would not extend the same help to trans women that they would to the rest of us . . .'

The three women seemed to be looking briefly at each other, making a silent decision about who was going to give me my answer.

'. . . so I was wondering what your position at RISE is. I will respect it either way. But I feel I have to make an active decision about it. Because the idea that not letting trans women into a shelter in case they somehow turn out to be some sort of bad apple seems unnecessarily punitive to me.'

A moment's pause.

'Alex, we are a women's shelter. And a women's shelter in Brighton. Of course we work with trans women. They are just as much at risk of violence in relationships as any of us are, on some occasions more so. And we work with all our guests on a case-by-case basis, assessing their needs individually. So the idea that one of our guests might be put into a vulnerable position by another who was a trans woman would not just be highly, highly unlikely, but also something that we could manage and avoid. So you can set your mind at ease.'

I felt as if my shoulders had dropped three inches. The relief! That there was, as I had hoped, a world of pragmatic women getting on with things, who had the data, who had the expertise, and who saw the faces on the women who turned up needing help. Who knew that to help trans women was the humane thing to do. While the columnists raged, the front-line staff were, as ever, taking care of business.

And the columnists had raged. From online writers with enormous followings to broadsheet journalists with huge readerships, there seemed to be an endless babble of opinion as the deadline for consultation regarding the government's proposed changes to the Gender Recognition Act approached. Some – men who spent an eye-watering number of hours per day on social media seething about the use of puberty blockers being akin to Josef Mengele's experiments – would have seemed laughable, pitiable even, if they hadn't been reaching such huge audiences. Others – the usual sort of attention-seeking populists from the tabloids who would have been saying that being gay 'is fine as long as you don't rub it in my face' a generation ago – were similarly infuriating but seemed like dinosaurs who would before too long be extinct.

But there were others who made my head spin with their relentless, almost obsessive writing about trans issues, despite the fact that they seemed to know no trans people and very little about their lives. Those who I had met, or interviewed, or whose work I had admired – left me gasping at the audacity of their claims. One assured me that at least one in fifty male prisoners identified as a trans woman, and responded with fury when I looked up two-month-old government statistics showing that it was a hundred and sixty-three women nationally.

The same arguments seemed to loop around the same relatively small group of largely white, well-salaried columnists. They seemed to be simultaneously arguing that non-gender conforming women were being 'forced' to transition in order to 'fit in' with society's norms, meaning that butch women were being erased and/or being called men, *and* that trans women cannot be real women because they are easily recognisable as 'men' from the angle of their jaw or shape of their arms. From time to time images of sports teams would bubble up on social media, with women debating the ones who were 'clearly' men. Those passing comment were so often the same women who were livid that tomboyishness was being expunged.

Then there were the arguments that puberty-blocking hormones – sometimes prescribed to adolescent children displaying signs of being trans – were taking a terrible toll on women's future fertility. The argument that our ovaries must be protected at all costs was now being made by the women I had grown up reading – sometimes in that locked cubicle in the military hospital – as they encouraged me to reach for the skies in my career rather than see motherhood as my lot. These were women whose words I had clung to as heartbreak had beset my twenties, who had encouraged me in my darkest times that my womb was not the only part of me which might produce something of value. And I had enjoyed their work again more recently, as I had undergone IVF and faced a future in which children might never happen after all. These words of solace about my value as a woman now seemed to have been replaced with the argument that these reproductive organs must be protected above all else, even if it meant entirely fragmenting a child's personality and sense of self.

Each time these debates resurfaced, conversations and columns would throw out a conciliatory mention of how the rising vitriol of the debate *did a huge disservice to the legitimate trans women out there* – without ever clarifying where the threshold of 'legitimate' lay for them. Was it that they had to be able to 'pass' as a woman when in public? Or did that make them all the more deceptive? Was it that they showed willingness, with hair and make-up, or did that just make them laughable? Was it that they had to have had the relevant surgeries, and if so – how far was far enough?

In my experience there are people who enjoy dancing on the edge of gender expectations, women who do not mind being mistaken for men, men who enjoy unleashing what some see as femininity: bold self-expression in a world which isn't always kind, no matter how you identify. Meanwhile there are others for whom gender identity *needs* to be met by appropriate gender expression, making medical intervention imperative. Just as there are some people for whom talking therapies, increased exercise and better diet are enough to creep out of a depression, while for others, drugs are a lifesaver.

Public debate seemed to have no space for individuals, for specifics or for the fact that all of us are messy, conflicted bundles of ego trying our best and often failing. Each time I saw one of these pieces, or caught the tail end of a 'debate' on social media, I would feel my adrenaline spike. I would decide not to read on, that it didn't matter. I would change L's nappy, read something else, make a cup of coffee. But inevitably I would go back and read it, my watch insistently beeping at me that my heart rate was raised. I would feel a rush of anger that people I knew and loved were being described in such terms. Then I would feel a rush of panic about whether to mention it to D in the spirit of solidarity or leave it unmentioned in the hope that she would be better off without seeing it. Then my worries would turn to the pragmatic. What would this mean for my family? How long until L could read something like this? How would it affect him in the long term?

What I found hardest was columnists who I had considered friends, who knew the reality of my situation – and had known D for years – who slowly phased me out. I had messaged one of them years earlier, inviting them down to talk to the steering group in Brighton council who had undertaken a city-wide Trans Needs Assessment body of research. '*These things are so much better discussed in person, with biscuits, I find*,' I had written. I received no reply.

And so, to be received with both warmth and pragmatism in this meeting had meant the world. I agreed to work with RISE on their forthcoming events, and even felt a little twinge of ambition that perhaps, later in the year, I might take part in one myself. As I left the building, I felt emboldened. How I lived from now on had to mean something positive. If the combined events of the last few years were going to be the axis upon which the second half of my life turned, then I wanted to make damn sure that it tipped in a direction I could be proud of. I had been through so much, my body had been through so much, but I was still in a position of such relative good fortune. Instead of feeling resentment or bitterness about the unravelling of my hopes and dreams for the next couple of decades, I began to see how much I had.

All I had ever wanted in life was to be average, to fit in. I had never wanted to win any marathons or to run the furthest, be the slimmest or go the longest. I had been proud of my averageness and spent years telling others that you didn't have to run to come first, that to be an ordinary runner was more than enough. Now, life had presented me with a turn of events which sat so far beyond 'average' that I had often felt completely adrift. I can never change what happened to my marriage. I may never be able to change the anti-trans sentiment that some people cling to. But what I can help to change is what is average. By being open and honest every day. By accepting my body for what it is, and all women's bodies for what they are. I am average, we are average. Perhaps together we can shift the mean.

11

The strides I had taken at creating a family in a new and unfamiliar shape were all well and good but as L's second birthday came and went, I still remained a new and unfamiliar shape. I had had to do so much mental processing, as well as the basic day-to-day business of caring for a toddler, that by the end of the year no matter what privilege I saw in my body, feeling *love* for it remained something of a stretch.

I still had patches of psoriasis, the legacy of my shingles, a pelvis that felt unsupported when I tried to do anything more than walk at pace, and a general sense of unease at living in a body that was still not working with me as much as I wanted it to. There had been so much else to do and think about that it seemed easier to simply not consider myself. The overthinking of D's body combined with the more toxic effects of Instagram meant I avoided the rubble of my physical self.

Over Christmas I mentioned to my brother W that I had long wanted to go to the Arctic Circle, and now had the excuse to do so because of a novel I had been commissioned to write. To my surprise, he was immediately keen to join me on the trip. Five years younger than me, he's a pretty shy person, not given to sudden impromptu promises. He had been very present, and very kind to me when things were at their hardest, but there is a limit to how much you can talk to your little brother about childbirth, marriage crises and baby poo, so perhaps we weren't as close as we had been at times. But something clicked that day, in the way that it can perhaps only do with siblings, and five months and several hundred WhatsApps later we were at Gatwick airport, ready for a twenty-four-hour journey north. He was on time, boarding passes printed and luggage packed like a pro. I was crouching by the scales at the check-in desk, frantically decanting some of the eight novels I had imagined I would read on our ten-day trip into his suitcase.

Somehow, micromanaging an infant's daily schedule and development had left me a flailing incompetent when it came to taking care of my own business if it didn't include a steriliser, a small Tupperware box of halved grapes or four muslins. My needs had so long been an afterthought that when they took centre stage I was, apparently, out of touch. As I clammily re-ordered my haphazard packing back into the suitcase, I sensed more than a little apprehension in my brother. More used to either business trips to the Far East or 'proper' travelling, the sort where a single rucksack could last months, ten far-flung days with an emotionally bruised older sister must suddenly have seemed less than appetising. Nevertheless, he hid it. Just about.

We flew to Trondheim, left our luggage locked at the station, and spent a rainy afternoon in the city, marvelling at the knit-wear, the coffee shops and the immaculate cycle paths. We schlumped around the grounds of its forbidding cathedral in the drizzle, killing time before our night train, more than a little apprehensive about the expedition ahead. Not long before midnight – and in what was still full daylight – we began our ten-hour journey along the Trondheim Fjord and beyond, into the Arctic Circle to a small town called Bodø. For the first hour or so, the corridors of the sleeper carriages were abuzz with people chatting, wandering up and down to get their bearings, and checking out the views. They were immediately spectacular: within minutes of leaving the station we were travelling along the edge of Trondheim Fjord, mere feet from the water's edge, the train's gentle chug-chug hugging the curve of the water.

After some initial hysteria as we struggled to access suitcases, brush teeth and put on pyjamas once our bunks had been unfolded, W and I wished each other goodnight. As I closed my eyes and felt the train's gentle lean back and forth, my body remembered the figure-of-eight motion I had used to rock newborn L to sleep in the small hours. I saw myself, holding him, just over two years earlier, shifting my weight from leg to leg and back and forth as my pelvis roared with pain and I tried to coax the tiniest burp from him. I watched us, my neck buried in his and vice versa, as we comforted each other, blissfully unaware of how much harder things were going to get. I had had so much hope in those early days: I had told myself I was going to do things so wonderfully, so full of patience, every decision considered with care. Instead, I had led us through the grimmest of times, operating a day, an hour, at a time as if scrabbling through a dark tunnel on hands and knees, just hoping that if we felt on a little further, the light might materialise.

Now, as I clutched my phone, already full of images D had sent me of the two of them at bathtime that evening, I wondered if we might at last be heading out of that tunnel. The train continued to lull me, and soon I was having my best night's sleep since early pregnancy.

We arrived in Bodø in time for a pleasingly traditional breakfast at the station. It was a modern building, the sort of forbidding post-war architecture that intimidates while also hinting at a sexy Cold War espionage drama. I was still dopey from almost too much sleep, overwhelmed by the snow-capped mountains surrounding the port, and made good use of the endless filter coffee in the station café.

We then caught a ferry for a few hours to the Lofoten Islands: a sprinkling of volcanic outcrops dotted along the Northern curve of Norway's coast. A spine of black rock plunging into blue water, punctuated by perfect Caribbean-white sandy beaches, eerie in their remote, imposing beauty.

We arrived, exhausted, just in time for the midnight sun. We were there during the period of the year when darkness never really falls, the sun staying in the sky throughout the night, casting an uncanny, relentless glare. We arrived at the guesthouse, quickly unpacked, then pottered around the small island we were staying on: only a few converted fishermen's huts, a restaurant and a closed-up kayaking business. We marvelled at how perspective seemed to shift and distort when everything was set against the shadow of huge slabs of granite mountain which looked as if they had been drawn by an angry graphic novelist. A little drizzle fell as we headed back to the guesthouse. I felt very far from home.

On our first morning we drove along the one single-lane road, and over the bridge which connected our island to the next, and visited the tourist information booth to check that the hikes we wanted to do were passable, and had reopened for the summer. It was late May, and the tourist season wouldn't start for a few weeks yet.

We meekly asked if the routes we wanted to take were hikes people like us might be able to manage, and the blonde woman peered briefly over the counter of her kiosk and gave us a cursory glance before shrugging and nodding, 'Sure,' with a slight smile. I felt rather flattered. We packed some sandwiches, some Aldi energy bars, and filled our water bottles before heading off for the foothills of Tindstinden, one of the southernmost mountains on Lofoten.

It was marked as 'moderate' in the guidebook we were using. A mere couple of kilometres. And it should take no more than an hour or two! The perfect starter climb, I told myself. Oh, how I had misunderstood the Scandinavian way with a hardy understatement. Sure, the climb was only a couple of kilometres, but within metres I realised that distance feels, well, it feels a little different when that distance is up and down rather than the smooth flat tarmac of the Brighton seafront. We were undeniably on a mountain. This wasn't the sort of hiking celebrities did when they went to Los Angeles, popped on a pair of Yeezys and took the wide, clear dust track up to the Hollywood sign for a couple of selfies. It was the sort of hiking that features in the first ten minutes of *Casualty*.

This was what I was thinking as I looked around (and, increasingly, up), but I didn't say anything for fear of worrying my brother. The last thing I wanted was him fretting about my well-being all the way up the mountain. Well, in truth, the last thing I wanted was him fretting about my well-being halfway up the mountain, and then deciding that things were 'too risky', that I might not 'be up to it' or that 'Mum and Dad would be furious if I let anything happen to you.' This was my kid brother, the little tyke who I had taught to make a bed, to use my tape deck, to ride a bike. I pretty much taught *him* to walk, I reminded myself. So there's no way I'm going to let him know how tough this seems.

There were, after all, stretches of the walk as we passed hidden lakes reminiscent of Cumbrian tarns, that were almost relaxing. From time to time we passed a small wooden hut perched lakeside, or spotted one peeking from the forest on an adjacent mountainside. In amidst the green, springy grass, clumped full of spongy moss, there was the odd wildflower – a hot pink here, a buttercup yellow there – which I would stop and photograph.

'I want to look it up later!' I'd cry ahead, secretly using the moments to catch my breath.

There were also stretches of the path which were not strictly 'path'. Nor walking, or even hiking, but climbing. The path would fade away as the mountainside steepened and the track turned into rudimentary stone steps half the size of our walking boots. We had to take it in turns, finding the small footholds in the rock face, shoving our boots as far as we could into the rock. Alongside these steeper parts were thick steel chains, running between steel posts which had been fastened into the mountainside. The steps, we quickly realised, were often too shallow to be safe without holding on to the chains to keep us steady. Hauling ourselves up, taking our bodyweight in our arms and pulling, was often easier than the thigh-work of taking such huge, steep strides.

My legs started to shake as we reached the third of these climbs. My core, so long a passenger, contributing nothing to my day-to-day use of my body, was suddenly having to hold itself firm as I steadied myself, occasionally veering from side to side as I misjudged the thickness or tautness of the steel chains. My ankles were trembling from nerves as much as the effort of holding myself stable, focusing on where I needed to tread next.

Then, just as my inner monologue was starting to lose its big-sister grit and wonder if perhaps I really wasn't up to this, we saw snow a few metres away. It was nearly June, but suddenly, huge fields of snow, nestled into the curve of the mountain, high up above a semi-frozen lake, were all revealing themselves ahead of us. We decided to keep going and to try and make it that far, if only to take some funny photos for family back home. The UK was apparently basking in a heatwave.

My heart was hammering in my chest. I had not felt this sensation of having to dig deep into my body's reserves since the first winter I had spent swimming year-round in cold water. That sensation of taking myself close to the edge of my capabilities, rather than being taken there by medicine or circumstance, was rushing back to me. What I had been experiencing emotionally, I now felt myself replicating in my body. Just try and find a foothold, only focus on the next one, don't look up and unnerve yourself with what might be coming next. I had spent so much of the last few years moving forward with similar trepidation.

As we had been walking, I had for the first time been explaining to my brother how things had slowly unravelled before suddenly collapsing, and how long and complicated the process of making sense of it all had been. The air grew colder, and the path twisted its way higher. I realised that this was the first time I had explained the whole story, from start to finish.

As we climbed, I started to describe how various parts of the hike were like my emotions during that period.

'That bit at the beginning when it looked flat, the section where the huge mountain behind disguised how steep the terrain we were on actually was – that was how the first few months after having L felt. I knew it was hard, I just couldn't work out why. The mountain in the distance was throwing my perspective.'

My brother nodded thoughtfully. He is an accountant. I suspect that ideally he would look for information about a climb from a map, not a series of metaphors about his sister's traumas. But it had been at least half an hour since we'd seen another hiker, and I had the thermos of coffee in my bag, so he was, in many ways, my hostage.

'Urgh, the bit with the steel chain to grab. That was the month I found out. Just tiny steps, clinging on by your toes while you felt yourself swaying around and hoping the wind didn't pick up. And you'd let go and fall if you stopped to think for a minute how far the drop was.'

'Sure, I get that,' he replied quietly.

'Then some of these bits, they're like the last six months or so. I can see the snow, right there in the distance, and I know it will be crisply refreshing! But bloody hell, the walk there seems to be going on a while. And I'm tired.'

'Uh-huh.'

And then, before we knew it, we had hit the snow. Crunchy, glittering. All around us. A huge flat field of it, hidden in the shadow of the mountain. Disorientating, but no more so than anything else in my recent past. I knew it was summer, and I knew it was early evening, but the sun was shining brightly above us and we were in a field of crisp white snow. I imagined L there, playing in it with me. I imagined his little legs, how they would be thigh deep in it. I longed to cuddle him, to show him how to make a snowball. But still I looked up, wincing at the dazzle of the sunlight, and took a deep breath. He was safe, he was loved. He was probably having a glass of milk and watching *Stick Man* at home with D right now. While here I was, my mind slowly loosening layer after layer of held-together, must-survive, let's-just-get-through-today-first determination. The simple process of moving my body, free from a buggy or an emergency or a deadline, had started to relax those coping mechanisms, to let me take a longer view, and to talk about it without fear of judgement. My brother, meanwhile, was undoing my rucksack and reaching for the coffee.

An hour later we reached the top, and were treated to views of the other islands along Lofoten's craggy spine, dotted off into the distance further north. We could see Bodø too. I felt so far away from L, hoped that he wasn't missing me too much, that perhaps he was too small to piece together how long I'd been gone. But I also felt closer to myself than I had since before he was born. When we got back to our rooms that night, I once again slept the sleep of the dead – despite the night never surrendering to anything like proper darkness.

The rest of the week continued in a similar vein. We walked, we talked, and we went to bed indecently early. Neither of us drank much more than a couple of glasses of wine, partly because of the prohibitive cost of alcohol in Norway, but also because it began to feel disrespectful to our bodies to be living so well all day and then to drink when we were already reeling with exhaustion.

Away from the television, away from my laptop, away from the minutiae of childcare – and in hours and hours of fresh air, tensions fell away. Slowly, the steady drop of cortisol which had been pumping into me for so long started to slow, its tap turning gently off. I realised that I was here, researching for new work, and that L was safe and loved at home with D. I was moving forward again. I could feel health, if not fitness, starting to flow back into my body.

On our last day, we had planned to take a boat trip, to treat ourselves and our legs a little easier after several days of hiking. But when we arrived at the small harbour, we were told by a fisherman busy unloading his cod that the boat had left already, having reached its maximum capacity of passengers earlier than expected.

'But when is the next one?' I asked, panicked.

'It runs once a day. There is no next one.'

My brother and I looked at each other. The next day we would be back on the train to Trondheim. What to do with the best part of a day in some small volcanic islands further north than Iceland?

Hike.

We took a deep breath and decided to have a shot at the one hike that neither of us had admitted to wanting to attempt. We had circled it in guidebooks, and picked up leaflets detailing its start point. But it was a challenging hike, and we had been worried that we were too tired, the weather might not hold, it wasn't worth doing just half the route and only seeing the summit but not the beach on the other side of the mountain. Now, however, there was little else left to do. So we did it.

We drove to the valley at the bottom of the mountain. Like so many of the islands in Lofoten this one had a wide flat valley full of lush grass and bright spring flowers in whites and yellows, beyond which lay huge peaks. The beaches snuggled into the curves of the mountains were particularly spectacular: white sand leading into neon-green water. The route itself was through a kilometre or so of lush valley and then up and over a peak. Yes, there was a fairy-tale beach on the other side of the peak, and yes, the only thing beyond it was the North Pole. But we would worry about that later. After all, we probably wouldn't make it.

The hike started off innocuously enough. There was a wooden boardwalk running straight through the field of ankle-deep wild flowers which led to the beginning of the hike up Ryten itself. The day was sunny, clouds rapidly being burned away as the heat increased, but the grass below the boardwalk was boggy from a long, dark winter. The view as we looked back was sublime, as the almost fake-looking lushness of the grass gently sloped away from the bottom of the mountain. Then, as I turned away from it, I looked up and realised just how far we had to go.

The grass was giving way to more rocky terrain, bits of volcanic ground sprouting where there had been flowers. The boardwalk was petering out. Now it was a case of looking down and concentrating every step of the way, making sure to find the flatter, more worn spots of rock, and making sure that you didn't place your foot on spongy grass which could give way to ankle-deep mud, or on a craggy section of rock on which your foot could twist and fall.

We were taking steep steps, using our quads to push us upwards as our hearts thundered faster and faster. The track wasn't as winding as some of the previous hikes we had done – it seemed to be heading straight upwards. Sweat was pouring down my back. Item by item, I was having to undress. First my woolly bobble hat. Then my scarf. Next, my coat. Then my long-sleeved top. I still couldn't quite see the summit.

The walk was starting to become boring. It was so steep that there was no view, and even on the odd curve where you might have had one, we had to keep our heads down, concentrating at all times on foot positioning. I was panting, my heart, lungs and muscles working harder together than they had done in years. The sensation of blood pressure and a hammering heart that might mean my head would burst clean off – that I had last felt shortly before arriving at hospital for my C section – was back, only this time it was warranted. I paused, gasping for air. The panicky sense of raw survival that I had spent all these months trying to creep away from was back. I wasn't a steely goddess capable of surviving anything. I wasn't a capable mother and decent friend. I wasn't an athlete, a sportswriter, an inspiration. I was just very tired and wanted a long nap in the sunshine, with no more foolhardy feats to deal with.

My brother, a little way ahead, looked back at me. I was doubled over, running my hands through my hair to regroup my ponytail as high as I could get it. I just wanted some breeze on the back of my neck and a glass of water. Please, no more.

'Come on, we're nearly there!' he cried back at me. 'You can do it!'

The idea was so silly that I didn't even bother to answer.

'I can see a couple posing for photographs so we must be near a view!'

But no, my legs and lungs said otherwise. It was just too much. It had all been too much, for too long. Suddenly I was as tired as I had ever been. Every night over the last two years that I had spent mulling, grieving, panicking, nursing, pacing, soothing and weeping caught up with me. My legs were lead, my heart on fire, my spirit gone. Please, no more ludicrous feats.

'No, I don't think I can do it,' I mumbled to myself. My hips ached from lifting them so high with each step up. The balls of my feet felt as flat as they had done on mile twenty of any marathon. My ankles were quivering as if I were on a high-wire.

What was the point anyway? I started to ask myself. *It's just another view.*

'Come on, YOU CAN DO IT!' yelled my brother. I don't know if it was the way the wind caught his voice, or the echoes of my former doubts swirling around my head as if I was out on those first marathon-training runs all over again, or if it was simply . . . genetics. But as his words reached me, I heard my father's voice. That infuriating belief in me, just when my own was crumbling.

My rage at his casual presumption that I would succeed was simmering. How *dare* he tell me what I was capable of? He didn't know if I could do it! And with that flick of the switch, the fury propelled me just far enough to see the couple he had been talking about. Yes, the summit was in sight. One big push, reminding my legs and lungs that there was always, always, that little bit more, and I caught my brother up.

We made it to the top, crept up to the small ledge the guidebooks had mentioned – where we took the obligatory photograph – then stepped back and let our breathing relax as we looked down onto the perfect beach below. The drop was vertiginous, several hundred metres of what wasn't a hike but a scrabble you'd have to do on hands and knees. But, confidence surging as I realised I could do so much more than I had remembered, I declared that it was no longer out of the question to climb down. We had come so far, we had nothing else to do all day – it wasn't as if it was going to get dark! We had food in our backpacks, we could see a stream heading straight down the mountainside towards the beach where we could fill up our water bottles. We had to do it. And so we did.

We scrambled down the side of the mountain, sweating like runners on mile twenty, hands clinging to clumps of grass to steady ourselves, knees trembling with the eternal pressure of steadying us again and again as we rattled down the mountainside, eventually making it to the beach. It was twice the size it had looked from almost a kilometre up. A huge flat crescent of dark volcanic sand giving way to dazzling blue water. I stripped off as fast as I could and headed towards the water, desperate to feel the cold contract my legs and feet. It was shallow for a good one hundred metres, barely reaching my thighs. And it was electric in its chill. I stood facing the Arctic and remembered the me who had pushed off that swimming-pool wall, promising herself, 'You're still you. You've still got you.'

I was. And I did. I had come through it. I felt like a building which had suffered a terrible fire. All paintwork, surfaces, ornament had gone, but the stone beneath still there, standing strong. Anything which didn't matter had simply burned away over those two years, but what remained was so solid I knew I could trust it. The sun blinked on the sea and I stared north. I returned home with more confidence than I had had for years.

We took the train back to Trondheim during the daytime. A glorious ten hours of the sort of views I had believed only existed on screensavers or jigsaw puzzles. Endless fjords, cabins and forests trundled past us, almost petulant in their endless gorgeousness.

'My eyes are full,' I declared about four hours in. 'I am trying to find a way to absorb some of it with . . . maybe my ears? Or hair? Can I use my hair to try and remember more of this beauty?'

I couldn't. But somewhere amidst the extremes of the natural world and the unflappable charm of the Norwegians, I had felt the *matryoshka* dolls of my fractured self slowly begin to reassemble. Parts of me which I had been at risk of forgetting – the silly, the carefree, the spontaneous – and parts of me I had sincerely believed were gone – the adventurous, the physically confident, the risk-taking – were starting to slide back into position, ready to let me be the self I had fought to be once again.

As I sat on that train, heading home to my toddler, to the new life I was building for us, I made two commitments to myself. I decided to give up alcohol for ninety days. Ten days in Norway had revealed – to my surprise! – that I didn't really enjoy drinking if I was relaxed already. I hadn't been consuming a lot before the trip (and had been a very occasional drinker during our IVF and my pregnancy), but for the last year or so, and particularly since D had moved out, I had been drinking consistently, just a couple of glasses of wine a night. It had ceased to become a pleasure and lapsed into a habit, as much to signify that it was time to relax as relaxing in itself.

I was also interested in unpeeling the layers of friendship to reveal who I simply saw socially, glasses in hands, chit-chat at the ready, and who were friends that would sit at ease with me while sober. Recent turbulence had already shone a medical-grade light onto my friendships, but I wanted to go a step further, particularly around work- and online-based friendships. I also wanted to remove that veneer of 'relaxation' from my evenings – which is when I did most of my mental churning. It was time to sit with those uncomfortable thoughts. It might be hard, but I suspected it would be worth it.

I was wrong. It wasn't hard. Within a week I felt clearer-headed than I had done for years. Within a month I looked clearer-headed than I had done for years. And after three months I realised that my relationship with alcohol was now changed for ever. I had thought that perhaps I didn't want to stop, pause and experience my emotions entirely without gloss, filter or analgesics. But it turned out I did. It turned out that at last I was ready to do so.

To have total mental clarity for an extended period of time proved enough to change a habit for good. More importantly, it gave me the emotional space – without the constant ticker tape of my conscience wondering, *Are you just feeling like this because you've had a glass of red?*, *Are you just overtired because you had a couple of glasses at that work thing last night?*, *Are you just anxious because you're still processing the consolatory wine someone bought you at lunch?* – to confront, and accept, the reality of my situation.

Months earlier, the fact that D and I had ever fallen in love would make me sob. Partly with shame, but also with the sheer weight of the grief. But now I swell with pride. I did fall in love. It was real, and the reasons it didn't work out were beyond painful. But I no longer feel as though it was all a mirage, or something of a failure. My love – our love – was what created the space in which D was able to come out. Without it, we would all be living in unimaginable pain and bringing L up from behind a facade of happiness. It took a sustained amount of time of full sobriety to recognise that, but to recognise it at last was sweeter than any cocktail.

The second commitment I made was to start working out again. Not running, not swimming, but doing proper workouts to strengthen my body in a specific and targeted way, from the core out. This was not about weight loss or leaner looks, it was about being able to literally hold myself up straight again. If I could feel that emotionally, I was doing myself a disservice if

I could not achieve it physically. For this, I knew I would need D's help. She had already been nothing but supportive with my sobriety mission, as she herself had all but given up alcohol. But regular gym attendance, to a specific schedule, required coordination and communication to make sure L's childcare ran as smoothly as possible. D did not hesitate. If that was what I needed to do, she would support it whenever her work permitted. This was just one of many compromises we were able to make with goodwill now that we were each living our lives as truthfully as we could.

So I joined a gym, doing a programme called F45 – a recommendation from my sister who had recently done the same, even longer after the birth of her two children. I felt like such a fraud on that first trip there. I was desperate that no one should recognise me, that no one might ask if was 'the one who wrote those sporty books'.

At first, I dreaded going. I even arrived dripping with sweat, wobbly-legged from the hilly cycle to the studio on my newly beloved second-hand bicycle. I felt lumpen and aged in comparison to some of the younger women in the class, and laughable compared to the men. But I persisted, and the more classes I attended, the more I realised that I was far from the oldest or the biggest – and that those were no bad things anyway.

Each class lasted for forty-five minutes, and I committed to attending five times a week, darting out of the door as D appeared to do bedtime for L, meeting her outside the gym to hand L over while they went to the nearby park together, and cycling at maximum capacity to the lunchtime classes on my two precious childcare days per week. Half of the classes were pure cardio, a special hell comprised of burpees, sprints and endless hops, skips and jumps – all timed to extract maximum effort with minimal recovery time. The other half was resistance based: lifting weights and using my own body as a weight to slowly, steadily build more muscle. All the instructors knew what my body had been through, kept a specific eye on the weaknesses in my back, and encouraged me to lift more and more with each passing week.

For so long I had hated the thought of heading to a gym, but this time, I found something which had been missing since my period in that hospital in Iserlohn: community. The gym was run by two women of around my age, and had a variety of instructors who were diverse in all sorts of ways. I discovered I had cold-water swimming in common with the intimidating guy whose background was boxing, another was a single mum who lived around the corner from me, and another was an LGBT+ ally from the very first moment I explained who I had just handed my toddler over to at the gym's reception. There were no twenty-year-old hot chicks Instagramming themselves doing squats, there were no men grunting as they slammed down the weights I was about to pick up, there was no sense that I was unwelcome.

Perhaps this was specific to me. Perhaps I had done enough mental hard work that I was simply ready to let myself fit in somewhere like this. Perhaps the decision to take action had been enough to make the action itself easier. Either way, it worked.

Slowly, my body began to respond to the exercise, and a body I recognised as mine started to emerge. As I tried for the hundredth time to do a press-up without my knees on the floor I remembered my time at the British Military Hospital. I was doing exercises so similar – some were identical – to those I had done twenty-five years previously, and again I was feeling healed by the experience.

I remembered the lessons about how new muscles are built, how in order to grow they need to be ripped so fresh blood can flow in. And how the term for making oneself stronger is Progressive Overload. As I watched sweat drip off the end of my nose and onto the mat for the twentieth time in a month, I realised that most of this strange time I had endured had been a case of progressive overload – me having to carry more and more, making further tiny rips, in order to ultimately re-emerge stronger. At last, my body was catching up with what my emotions had been up to all along.

After a few weeks I realised that my stroke on the rowing machine had changed: when I pulled back, legs extended, I could suddenly reach a further two inches. There was simply less of me around my waist. But instead of feeling lesser, as I had always dreaded whenever I lost weight, when my hands hit my core it felt strong. It felt as if it were supporting my back, supporting me, holding me together. Doing the exercise has not 'given me my body back': I always knew it was mine. I had just felt utterly disconnected from it, and exercise has helped reconcile my mental and physical selves. Only a couple of inches away lies my uterus, its strange shape still there, still hidden. But now, instead of representing danger to me, it makes me feel proud that L and I both made it. Because just when I thought I had lost so much of myself,

I discovered an ability to regain strength where I believed there was none left.

A couple of years ago it seemed that there was no longer room in my own life for me to be me. I had been pressed to the very edges of my own experiences by what so often seemed to be far bigger forces at play, left gasping for a little oxygen in what seemed such a crowded space. Perhaps that is why I neglected to reconnect with my own body for so long: there were days when I felt I needed to remind myself that it was OK to have a body, and to take up any space at all.

A dissociation after trauma, serious illness or even sudden weight change is common. But so is the disassociated way that so many of us view ourselves from the outside in, dwelling on how we present to the world, to others rather than to ourselves. Of course for some, how we present can literally be what places us in danger: the trans person who does not 'pass', the black man who is deemed 'threatening', the injured face which others find frightening. For these individuals, society's gaze is justifiably anxiety-inducing, as it can and does result in physical harm. For the rest of us, this relentless appraisal from the outside in is exhausting, but usually little more than that. What luxury. And as I discovered, when you shift your perspective to focusing on how you see the world rather than how it sees you, and realise the good fortune of having this choice in the first place, it makes that shift far easier to make. Remembering this was a good first step for me. And exercise an excellent second one. Working out alone could not shift this dissociation, but it was an essential part of my recovery. Feeling the blood charge through my veins, feeling the sweat drip, feeling an engagement with nature and the animal self I had felt so far apart from during pregnancy and childbirth. We are not living our fullest if we are not enjoying our bodies, any more than we are our best selves if we prioritise our bodies above all else, ignoring the emotions that arise in our physical selves too.

I have had to challenge myself in ways I didn't know were possible. I have climbed mountains, literal and emotional. I had to look at what it is to be a woman, in a female body. I had to look at other women, and what the bodies they live in meant to me. And I had to look at what equality means, and where all of our different needs intersect.

I am not immune to the disadvantages of being born with a woman's body. The physical disadvantages in a world often literally designed for the able-bodied white male. The sexual politics, the burdens put on us by childbirth and child-rearing, the pay disparity, the structural inequalities in the courts and beyond. But I am also aware of the huge honour it is to be born into a beautiful, healthy, adaptable body which I recognise as mine, for me. When I chose to get stronger, I could. When I chose to dig deeper, I could. When I chose to climb mountains, I could.

Now I can get on with the second half of my life. My midpoint pivot was sharper than many of us experience, but in so many ways that proved to be a blessing. I plan to be in this body for many years, decades more! It is no longer as lithe as it once was, and it won't always be as strong as it still is. I will watch it age and weaken in time, but I now know two things more keenly than ever before. First, that I am lucky to have this body. The joy it has given me far outweighs the pain. And second, that it wasn't my body, or even my husband's, I was grieving for – it was my connection with myself. I don't want to feel obliged to love my body without question, I don't want to feel obliged to shape it to suit fashion. I simply want to feel connected to it, informed by it and supported by it. As with all the most important relationships in my life, I don't want to be defined by it, but I do want to feel that I am in partnership with it.

But now I also know that there is space in that equation to support other women and their bodies – whatever their shape or size. Last month I took part in my first running event for five years. After months of working out, I finally dared to try running again, only to find myself faster and stronger than I had been since getting married. The event was only an eight-kilometre race along the cliffside in Brighton, but it was the furthest I had run since starting IVF. It was to raise funds for RISE, the charity I have now been working with since that first meeting, including hosting their twenty-fifth anniversary celebrations – an event I will never forget.

My sister came down for the weekend to run alongside me, and we were accompanied by two other friends who knew what the event meant to me. It was a stormy morning, full of bluster, the sea winds whipping our hair into our faces as we walked to check in our bags at the registration area. I was as nervous as I had been at my first running event; it was as if I had never run a step in my life as we did some warm-up exercises in the shelter of the cliffside, the music blaring, foil blankets flapping in the breeze. I felt sick with nerves – not just about whether I could run the distance, but about whether that solace, that glee, that sense of truly living in my body would be there when we set off.

The group headed out along the shoreline and as ever it took time for my heart rate to find its balance, working alongside the beat of my feet. The panic subsided and I started to recognise feelings I had for so long left behind me. The sense that keeping going would keep me going. The sense that all I had to do was have faith and follow the path. The sense that, surrounded by others – such a variety of ages, shapes and sizes – I wasn't alone. I willed myself onwards, looking forward to having the wind behind me as I turned at the four-kilometre point and headed back to the finish line. But, when I reached halfway and headed back, I realised I had in fact turned into the wind. It was lashing at my face, slapping my ponytail into my eyes, seemingly pushing me back the further I pressed on. It was a fight to reach the finishing line, and I had to run harder than I ever had before. But I made it, and immediately burst into tears.

I was still me. I was still there. I had been there all along. And now I was not just free, but strong enough to enjoy it.

Yes, the events of the last few years were a trauma that took time to recover from. But now that I'm tougher, I know that the story of my marriage can make for quite the anecdote: I can pull focus, confounding people's expectations of me if I feel patronised. The women and children I interviewed on stage at the RISE anniversary event are in an entirely different category. Survivors of domestic abuse and coercive control read their stories for us to listen and bear witness to; children I had met at the shelter during the summer had their moment on stage talking about what a move of city had done for them; and women who had run the service for decades talked about their work and what it meant. These are the women I wish I had known about during my darkest hours. In the survivors and staff alike there is a combined tenacity which allows them to stare the very worst of times in the face and deal with it, and a sense of hope that we have the potential to help each other to live better, freer lives.

Working with RISE has changed my outlook on what women are capable of – both in terms of survival and what they can offer other women. I hope that they will have me as long as I am useful to them, but in the meantime it has become a Christmas tradition that D and I donate to the charity on each other's behalf instead of bothering with Christmas gifts. It is a sweet relief to know that I am finally doing something D will truly appreciate after years of watching her not know how to respond to the jumper, the scarf or the dressing gown that I didn't yet know was entirely inappropriate. This Christmas we came full circle, and I finally felt strong enough to spend it with D. Of course L loved every minute of it, but then he loves any room with Lego, snacks and either of us in it. He is the gift we never thought we would receive, and to celebrate with him felt like peace at last. One day, I will find romantic love again. To be at peace with my little family finally gave me the confidence to believe in that. Just because there is scar tissue, doesn't mean there isn't strength, flexibility, optimism about how much more there is out there to be enjoyed.

The morning after L's birth, a nurse appeared at my bedside, announcing that it was time to help me stand for the first time since I had been helped onto the hospital bed twenty-four hours earlier, ready to receive my anaesthetic.

'Try to focus on your feet,' she told me. It seemed perplexingly obvious advice. But I gently inched my legs around to the side of the bed, grasping her forearms as she grasped mine, and within seconds I understood what she meant: as I stood, finally vertical, I felt my internal organs slide as they rearranged themselves in my now so much emptier abdomen. That eerie sensation of my innards reformatting themselves, of the fading numbness of anaesthetic slowly leaving my body, was something I had expected to last for little more than a few more hours.

Instead, it seems that I needed it to last a bit longer. Only very recently does that inner rearrangement seem to have reached its conclusion, and that emotional anaesthesia to be wearing off. It took years to feel as if once again I fitted back inside my own skin. It was a battle. A war. A growing up.

Yesterday I took L swimming for the first time after a few months of winter colds and vomiting bugs. I wasn't sure how long we'd last, if his nervousness would be back. But for the first time ever, he walked into the gently sloping water without holding my hand. He didn't look back, but kept wading until the water was well above his midriff. Then, instinctively, he pushed off from the pool's blue tiled floor and began to swim, neither of us quite able to believe it. The weightlessness, the freedom, the joy washed over him as he realised he could kick and turn to face me, shouting, 'Mummy, what's me do?!'

'You're doing it!' I cried back as he floated towards me, toes pointed, arms wide, pure pleasure beaming from his face. 'You can do it! You see how brave you were, you did it even after all the times you were scared!'

ACKNOWLEDGEMENTS

There are so many people I would like to thank, not just for their help with the writing of this book, but for their support and goodwill during what came first: the living of it. The British Transport Police officers who took such good care of me in March 2017; the court volunteer at Brighton Magistrates Court who showed me such kindness; and the woman who came forward at the time, made herself available to the police while on holiday and then returned to court as a witness. The Agora Clinic in Hove, particularly Carole Gilling-Smith, who stepped up with astonishing warmth and professionalism when I needed them. And Professor Kypros Nicolaides and the team at the Fetal Medicine Centre for their attentive care during my strange and specific crisis. I am also hugely grateful to the team at the Royal Sussex County Hospital in Brighton, particularly Dr Praneil Patel: despite the chaos I was in, I could not have wished for a calmer or more positive birth.

Writing this book was at times very challenging, and I owe a huge amount to the patience and wisdom of Becky Hardie at Chatto and Sarah Ballard at United. Your clarity of thought when I had none, your respect for my story and your faith in my ability to tell it were reassuring and inspiring in equal measure.

I am for ever indebted to my friends and family: they provided me with not only comfort, consolation and company when I was at my very lowest, but then quietly let me forget further birthdays and anniversaries while I wrote the book. As I write this in May 2020, I am very, very much looking forward to making this up to you in person.

But it is my local friends – the boots on the ground – to whom I owe the most thanks. Friends who checked in on me while pretending they weren't, fed me when I didn't know what to eat, and made me laugh when I was worried that I might be forgetting how to do it. Damian Barr, John Campbell, Katherine Fraser, David Gilmour, Euan MacDonald, Joe Minihane, Lucy Moses, Mike Moran, Jack Ruston, Jessica Ruston, Polly Samson, Mary Kate Trevaskis, Emily Williams-Seymour: you were in uncharted territory with me, and I am for ever grateful for your companionship.

I would also like to thank the team at RISE (https://www.riseuk.org.uk/), particularly Nicola, for welcoming me into their community and letting me hear and share so much about what they do. Their work, and the women that they work with, are an ongoing inspiration – especially you, Lacey!

And D, thank you for not just encouraging me to tell my story, but for working so hard with me to create an ending this happy. Onwards, with joy!